how good is your Pot-Limit Hold'em?

Stewart Reuben

NB

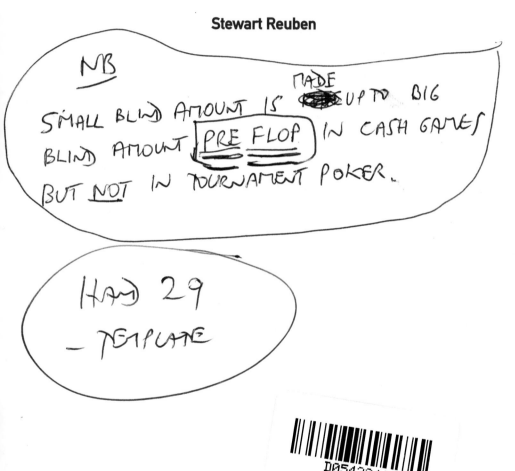

SMALL BLIND AMOUNT IS MADE UP TO BIG BLIND AMOUNT PRE FLOP IN CASH GAMES BUT NOT IN TOURNAMENT POKER.

HAND 29
– TEMPLATE

First published in 2004 by D & B Publishing, PO Box 18, Hassocks, West Sussex BN6 9WR

Reprinted 2004

British Library Cataloguing-in-Publication Data
A catalogue record for this book is available from the British Library.

ISBN 1-904468-08-X

All sales enquiries should be directed to:
D & B Publishing, PO Box 18, Hassocks, West Sussex BN6 9WR, UK
Tel: 01273 834680, Fax: 01273 831629, e-mail: info@dandbpublishing.com,
Website: www.dandbpublishing.com

Dedicated to David Moskovic.

Cover design by Horacio Monteverde.
Production by Navigator Guides.
Printed and bound in United States by Versa Press Inc.

Contents

Acknowledgements

I would like to thank Dr Mahmood Mahmood and his wife, as well as Andrew Kinsman and Byron Jacobs for their valuable advice and encouragement.

Danny Copeland and David Moskovic tested most of the quizzes in this book. Their scores are shown in the scorecharts.

Recommended Further Reading

Championship No-Limit and Pot-Limit Hold'em by T.J. Cloutier with Tom McEvoy (Cardsmith 1997)

How Good is Your Pot-Limit Omaha? by Stewart Reuben (D&B Publishing 2003)

Pot-Limit and No-Limit Poker by Bob Ciaffone and Stewart Reuben (Bob Ciaffone 1999)

The Science of Poker by Dr Mahmood N. Mahmood (High Stakes 2003)

Starting out in Poker by Stewart Reuben (Everyman 2001)

Super/System – A Course in Power Play by Doyle Brunson et al (B&G Publishing 1978)

Tournament Poker for Advanced Players by David Sklansky (Two Plus Two Publishing 2002)

Introduction

It is now around 50 years since *How Good is Your Chess?*, a popular form of chess instructional material, was pioneered by Leonard Barden. In *How Good is Your Chess?* the reader was invited to take an imaginary seat next to a grandmaster in a recent game and deduce each of his next moves, scoring points (or losing them!) according to the accuracy of their answers. At the conclusion of the game the reader was then instructed to tot up their score, and see how well they had fared, using a scorechart provided by the author.

I first had the kernel of the idea of writing a poker book along these same lines some years ago. Fellow chessplayers and the editors of this series, Byron Jacobs and Andrew Kinsman, came up with the idea independently. *How Good is Your Pot-Limit Omaha?* was the first fruit of our discussions, and this book is a companion volume.

The book comprises 58 hands, each of which contains numerous questions for you to answer. In order to get the most out of this book, it is recommended that you work your way through all of the questions for each hand before checking any of the answers. You should not assume that the player of the hand, often myself, made the optimal choice. In this way you will come to each decision 'cold' and will avoid receiving any hint which will help you to answer the remaining questions in the hand. Thus, as far as possible, the play will follow that of a 'live' hand. The analysis of each hand appears at its conclusion.

Hold'em is a much purer form of poker than Omaha. Unlike Omaha, where two players may have hands of virtually equal merit, one with a good made hand and the other with a big draw, in hold'em one player almost invariably has the better hand. In Omaha, there are many purely technical matters to consider, whereas hold'em often boils down to taking a view – which is quintessentially what poker is all about.

Hold'em is mainly played in two ways for money, limit and pot-limit. No-limit cash games are seen relatively rarely these days. It is too easy to smother the drawing hand by over-betting the pot. However, many tournaments are played no-limit. The strategy of playing a no-limit tournament is of a quite different nature to a pot-limit cash game. Casinos tend to prefer no-limit tournaments because it is easier to ensure they reach an early conclusion. They also prefer pot-limit to no-limit cash games because players do not go broke so rapidly. The casinos make their money from table charges and rakes in cash games, so it is not in their interests for players to take an early bath.

The cards and the players may be the same, but the play can be quite different; depending on whether the game is tournament or cash. I know of some players who only play in cash games, and others who play exclusively in tournaments. This seems to me to be a mistake, since both forms are perfectly valid.

Then there are satellite tournaments, in which perhaps ten players all put up the same sum and, when the dust has settled, there is just one player standing. That player then wins a place in the main tournament. Such events often take a couple of hours from start to finish. The main tournament is different as usually more than one place is paid. Another form, another strategy.

To play all the different types of game requires considerable flexibility. That is why we meet so few players who are uniformly successful. This book concentrates on pot-limit hold'em.

My book on pot-limit Omaha was principally set around hands I either played or saw take place in 2002-2003. Except where I have dabbled on the Internet and now one tournament, I have not played any hold'em for some years. You will find that some hands in this book date back a very long way indeed.

As I pointed out in the companion book, the mere act of discussing a particular hand changes the goalposts. You are alerted to the fact that there is something of interest. Life is somewhat different in the hurly-burly of a cardroom with money being splashed in the pot and everybody out to get you. Perhaps pure analysis is more suited to games played on the Internet. That is no bad thing; online poker is growing even as I write these words.

In this book standard poker notation is used, most of it which is completely self-evident. It is just necessary for me to point out that A-X denotes an ace with any sidecard and ?-? and K-? indicate that you have no knowledge of both or just one of your cards respectively. An 's' is used to denote two cards of the same suit.

Read and enjoy. Remember that even if you do not want to test yourself, there will be much to learn from our hands. Some of the things that I have learnt in writing this book have been a revelation to me.

Some of the hands are partly analysed with fairly complex arithmetic. I know this is a big turn-off for some. Thus there is a government health warning at the start of such sections, in the form of a skull and crossbones.

WARNING: Complex maths follows

David Moskovic tested himself on a number of these questions and his scores are shown in the scorecharts. At the time he had been playing poker for about 18 months. He has also helped in correcting many errors; those that remain are all my responsibility. Danny Copeland is even less experienced, and his scores are also shown.

Stewart Reuben,
London,
January 2004

Ranking of Starting Hands

On page 26 of my book, *Starting out in Poker*, I gave a list of the order of merit of poker hands before the flop. This developed from David Sklansky's similar list in *Hold'em Poker*. Mine was for all forms of poker, whereas we are dealing solely with pot-limit here. There seems to be no advantage in changing the list. After all, it is just a matter of opinion. Perhaps pairs should be valued more highly, and perhaps A-K is a more potent weapon in tournaments.

Just because a hand is higher up the list than another, does not imply that is favourite in an all-in coup. J♠-2♣ is a 54%-46% favourite over 10♥-9♦ in an all-in coup. But the former hand does not even merit consideration in the list, whereas 10-9 is in Group 7.

The middle column denotes the group to which each hand belongs. The strategy for playing hands in the same group can be very similar.

'Odds' represents the odds of receiving this hand or better.

s is used to denote two cards are of the same suit.

X stands for a card of undefined denomination.

Other hands are hardly worth considering. Thus their relative merits are of no interest. If you choose to play them, effectively you are bluffing. Since nobody knows your hand anyway, what is the point? There is no need to saddle yourself with poor starting hands. The following list contains enough choice for all your bluffs.

Ranking of Starting Hands

	Hand	Group	Odds		Hand	Group	Odds
1.	**A-A**	1	220/1	**37.**	**Q-10**	7	3.5/1
2.	**K-K**	2	110/1	**38.**	**K-10**	7	3.5/1
3.	**Q-Q**	2	73/1	**39.**	**10-9**	7	3.5/1
4.	**A-Ks**	2	60/1	**40.**	**9-8**	7	3/1
5.	**A-K**	2	38/1	**41.**	**8-7**	7	3/1
6.	**A-Qs**	3	34/1	**42.**	**7-6**	7	3/1
7.	**A-Js**	3	31/1	**43.**	**6-5**	7	3/1
8.	**J-J**	3	27/1	**44.**	**5-4**	7	2.5/1
9.	**K-Qs**	3	25/1	**45.**	**A-X**	8	2/1
10.	**A-Q**	3	20/1	**46.**	**10-8s**	8	2/1
11.	**A-10s**	4	19/1	**47.**	**Q-8s**	8	2/1
12.	**10-10**	4	17/1	**48.**	**J-8s**	8	2/1
13.	**K-Q**	4	14/1	**49.**	**K-Xs**	8	1.5/1
14.	**A-Xs**	4	12/1	**50.**	**J-9**	8	1.5/1
15.	**K-Js**	4	11/1	**51.**	**Q-9**	8	1.5/1
16.	**Q-Js**	5	11/1	**52.**	**K-9**	8	1.5/1
17.	**9-9**	5	10/1	**53.**	**Q-8s**	8	1.5/1
18.	**A-J**	5	9/1	**54.**	**J-7s**	8	1.5/1
19.	**J-10s**	5	9/1	**55.**	**9-7s**	8	1.5/1
20.	**K-10s**	5	8.5/1	**56.**	**8-6s**	8	1.5/1
21.	**8-8**	5	8/1	**57.**	**7-5s**	8	1.5/1
22.	**K-J**	5	7.5/1	**58.**	**6-4s**	8	1.5/1
23.	**Q-J**	5	7/1	**59.**	**4-3s**	8	1.5/1
24.	**10-9s**	5	6.5/1	**60.**	**5-3s**	8	1.5/1
25.	**A-10**	6	6/1	**61.**	**J-8**	9	1.5/1
26.	**Q-10s**	6	6/1	**62.**	**Q-8**	9	evens
27.	**small pair**	6	5/1	**63.**	**10-8**	9	evens
28.	**9-8s**	6	5/1	**64.**	**9-7**	9	evens
29.	**8-7s**	6	5/1	**65.**	**8-6**	9	evens
30.	**7-6s**	6	4.5/1	**66.**	**7-5**	9	evens
31.	**6-5s**	6	4.5/1	**67.**	**6-4**	9	evens
32.	**5-4s**	6	4.5/1	**68.**	**4-2s**	10	evens
33.	**K-9s**	7	4.5/1	**69.**	**3-2s**	10	evens
34.	**J-10**	7	4/1	**70.**	**10-7**	10	evens
35.	**J-9s**	7	4/1	**71.**	**K-X**	10	3/4
36.	**Q-9s**	7	4/1	**72.**	**others**	11	certain

Hand 1

Exploding a Myth

♣ – ♥ – ♦ – ♠ – ♣ – ♥ – ♦ – ♠

INTRODUCTION

Pots are smaller in hold'em than in Omaha. Thus, to produce comparable action, it is necessary to have higher blinds. In England it is quite common to play a round of Omaha followed by a round of hold'em. The problem with this is that the blinds must be the same, which automatically means that the Omaha rounds will be bigger.

The game is £1000 buy-in pot-limit hold'em with blinds of £25-£50. (Unless otherwise stated, there are nine players in all the hands in this book.) The small blind, Al has gone £25 and the big blind, Joe £50. Everyone has passed to you and you are last on the button.

You hold ?-?. That's right. You have not looked at your hole cards yet. I advise against this type of play. If someone raises immediately in front of you, then you should look at your hand, and now all eyes will be trained on you and your action. Inevitably you will sometimes make an inadvertent gesture that gives the game away. It is much better to look at your hand while others are acting. The trick is to do this while at the same time observing the reactions of the other contestants.

The pot stands at £75. It is £50 to you.

THE PLAY

Question 1: Should you: (a) pass (b) call (c) raise £50 (d) raise the maximum £150? (Although there is only £125 in the pot after you call £50, in some games you are allowed to raise as if the small blind had already called. Thus the maximum raise here is to £200 total.)

(a) ☐	(b) ☐	(c) ☐	(d) ☐	Points: ....

Action: You make it £200 to go. Al passes in the small blind and Joe calls in the big blind. The pot stands at £425.

Flop: 9♠-5♦-3♦. Joe checks to you.

Question 2: Should you: (a) check (b) bet £150 (c) bet £400?

(a) ☐	(b) ☐	Points: ....
		Total: ....

Action: You bet £400. Joe passes and you have made £225 in total ignorance of your holding. Before you start congratulating yourself, remember that you did put £600 at risk!

WARNING: Complex maths follows

It would be much more dangerous to try this tactic at pot-limit Omaha, since Al and Joe are each going to call you about 50% of the time. Thus you will win 25% of the hands unchallenged, 50% of the time one or other player will call and 25% of the time they will both call. Oops, I forgot something – it is quite possible that either Al or Joe will reraise you!

In hold'em, each player should call when they at least hold something in the top one-third of starting hands. Thus each of Al and Joe will pass 67% of the time. Now you will win 67% x 0.67, or about 45% of the hands unchallenged.

You have relied completely on your positional advantage here. Despite the fact that this play is much weaker in Omaha, Bob Ciaffone, in his otherwise excellent book *Omaha Holdem Poker – The Action Game*, categorically states on page nine that, 'Acting last is a stronger advantage at Omaha than any other game, and that player does not need any additional incentive to enter the pot.' This is flatly wrong. In Omaha, an opponent does not need a good made hand to call, as long as he has a reasonable draw. The holding 7♠-6♦-5♦-3♣ is clearly not winning, but its win potential is high and the likelihood of becoming heavily involved, and losing, is small.

Anyway, you won the hand on this occasion and I am not going to let you in on the secret of your own hole cards. How could I? I don't know what they were!

SCORECHART

20 Well done, you obviously understand hold'em is about what your opponents may have, not what you actually hold. David and Danny both scored full marks.

12-19 That's fine.

5-11 You really should not be a happy bunny at this stage of reading the book.

0-4 An ugly score indeed.

ANSWERS AND ANALYSIS

Holding: ?-?.

Answer 1: (a) -5 (b) 4 (c) 2 (d) 10.

It would be crazy to pass blind. Calling blind is rather odd, but there you are. Normally you would look at your cards and make a rational decision. You are not being afforded that luxury on this occasion. You intend to bluff, or at least try to. After all, you may have a pair of aces. One important thing though, you must make certain that no-one is aware that you are raising blind!

Flop: 9♠-5♦-3♦.

Answer 2: (a) 0 (b) 4 (c) 10.

Whatever hand you may have, it is unlikely that this flop will have helped Joe. The only reason you might want to sneak a peek at your cards, is that you may prove to be very strong and want to give a free card.

Hand 2

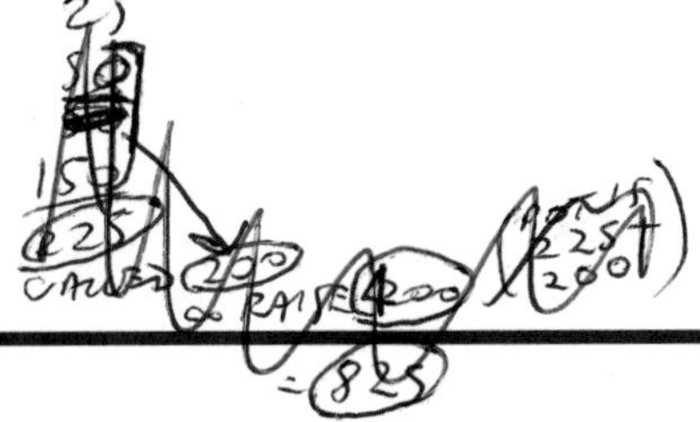

Implied Odds

INTRODUCTION

Again the game is £1000 buy-in with £25-£50 blinds. Al is in the small blind and Joe in the big blind. Everyone has passed to you on the button, but this time you decide to sneak a peek at your cards. You hold 8♣-7♣.

THE PLAY

Question 1: Should you: (a) pass (b) call (c) raise £50 (d) raise £150?

(a) ☐	(b) ☐	(c) ☐	(d) ☐	Points: ....

Action: You make it £200 to play. Al passes and Joe raises £400. Perhaps he has realised that you are always beating up on him in this position and has decided to make a stand. It is essential to vary your play. The pot stands at £825.

Question 2: When both of you have £5000 left, should you: (a) pass (b) call (c) raise £400 (d) raise £1200?

(a) ☐	(b) ☐	(c) ☐	(d) ☐	Points: ....

Question 3: Same question, but you each have £20,000 left?

(a) ☐	(b) ☐	(c) ☐	(d) ☐	Points: ....

Action: Both of you have £20,000 so you decide to call on this occasion. There is £1225 in the pot.

Flop: Q♥-7♠-2♦. You hold 8♣-7♣. Joe bets £1000. This is no surprise, since the last raiser will normally bet the flop in hold'em, and this flop looks extremely innocuous. The pot stands at £2225.

Question 4: Should you: (a) pass (b) call (c) raise £1000 (d) raise £3200?

(a) ☐	(b) ☐	(c) ☐	(d) ☐	Points: ....

Action: You call. The pot stands at £3225.

Hypothetical Turn: Q♥-7♠-2♦-9♥. You hold 8♣-7♣. You each have £18,600 left. Joe bets £2000 and the pot stands at £5225.

Question 5: Should you: (a) pass (b) call (c) raise £2000 (d) raise £7200?

(a) ☐ (b) ☐ (c) ☐ (d) ☐ Points: ....

Action: You pass and we get on with the next hand. Whatever happened to your implied odds? You have lost the original £400 plus £1000 more.

Now let us go back to the actual hand:

Turn: Q♥-7♠-2♦-8♥. You hold 8♣-7♣. You each have £18,600 left. Joe bets £2000 and the pot stands at £5225.

Question 6: Should you: (a) pass (b) call (c) raise £2000 (d) raise £7200?

(a) ☐ (b) ☐ (c) ☐ (d) ☐ Points: ....

Action: You raise £6600 and Joe calls. The pot now stands at £20,425.

River: Q♥-7♠-2♦-8♥-A♣. You hold 8♣-7♣. There is £10,000 left to bet. Joe bets £8000.

Question 7: Should you: (a) pass (b) call (c) raise £2000 all-in?

(a) ☐ (b) ☐ (c) ☐ Points: ....

Action: You call and he turns out to have K-Q. Phew! He has played badly. After all, it is highly possible that you yourself could have had A-Q. He should have passed on the turn. The final pot is £36,425.

You have won £18,425 for your £400 risk before the flop. This is 46/1 for your money. That is an expression of your implied odds on this particularly occasion. However, before you pat yourself on the back, remember that you had to outdraw Joe on the turn.

Hypothetical Action: Joe checks on the river. The pot is £20,425 and there is £10,000 left to bet.

Question 8: Should you: (a) check (b) bet £2000 (c) bet £5000 (d) bet £10,000 all-in?

(a) ☐ (b) ☐ (c) ☐ (d) ☐ Points: ....

Total: ....

Action: You check and show your two pair. Joe stares and stares and eventually throws away his hand. Why do people do that? They can hardly be savouring the moment of truth. No, they must think that they are on television.

This time you won £10,425 for that £400 outlay. This is 26/1 for your £400 risk when you called Joe's pre-flop raise.

Think of the danger you have exposed your money to. Was it worth it? Did your blood pressure go sky-high? Note the huge amount of money you must play for in order to justify that call at the outset.

SCORECHART

80 Well done. Of course, you won't have won the most money!

70-79 An excellent mix between aggressive and solid play.

55-69 I scored 64 and David 61.

40-54 This is beginning to be uneasy. You need more experience. Danny scored 45.

25-39 You should not be playing poker for money that hurts you when you lose.

2-24 Carry on reading.

ANSWERS AND ANALYSIS

Holding: 8♣-7♣.

Answer 1: (a) 0 (b) 10 (c) 3 (d) 5.

There are far worse hands than this in poker. However, it is a playing hand and it would be a pity to raise and then be taken off the hand due to a big reraise. On the other side of the coin, you won comfortably in the same situation in Hand 1.

Answer 2: (a) 10 (b) 0 (c) 0 (d) 0.

Answer 3: (a) 10 (b) 3 (c) 0 (d) 0.

It is hardly feasible that you are winning this hand. However, it is one that plays well. For one thing, it is extremely easy to pass if the flop misses you completely. You must also consider your implied odds – the amount that you could win if your ship comes in. It is received wisdom that you should not commit more than 5% of your chips in such situations. If you can only win £5000 for the £400 risk, that is 12.5/1. However, if you can win £20,000, that is 50/1. Therefore a call can be countenanced only in the second instance.

If you are going to play this type of hand, then 8-7 is in some ways a better holding than 10-9. It is less likely that 8-7 will be dominated by your opponent holding a hand such as 9-8. With 10-9, you may well be dominated by J-10 or A-10. But passing is still the safer option. I give a score of three points for the call in the large stack scenario. In a way that can be used as a guide to how often you should do make this play; one in three hands feels about right.

Before you embarked on your raise, you should have already decided what you would do if either player were to raise back. A rapid, confident call will suggest that you have a fairly strong hand.

Flop: Q♥-7♠-2♦.

Answer 4: (a) 2 (b) 10 (c) 3 (d) 0.

Well, what were you anticipating on the flop? Even hitting a pair is better than you would expect. You may or may not be winning. If you flat call and the turn card is low, then Joe will probably check if he has nothing. (Of course, you must realise that he may also check with a very strong hand!) Anyway, you then bet and he may well pass. Limping in for £1000 will only go wrong if he happens to get lucky and outdraw you.

Answer 5: (a) 10 (b) 0 (c) 3 (d) 1.

Unless Joe has cracked up, he must have something. It could, for example be K-K or just a queen. If you opted to raise then I admire your *chutzpah*, but probably not your bank balance. At least that would be better than lamely calling in a pot-limit game.

Turn: Q♥-7♠-2♦-8♥.

Answer 6: (a) 0 (b) 5 (c) 0 (d) 10.

You have hit a major hand and it is time to make the most of it. Clearly Joe has something. Of course, if his holding is Q-Q then you are going to go seriously broke with no outs whatsoever. Naturally you may prefer a call and then, when a blank comes, and Joe checks, bet the pot. Certainly, if you play that way and a queen or deuce comes on the river instead, then you can comfortably pass if Joe bets.

River: Q♥-7♠-2♦-8♥-A♣.

Answer 7: (a) 10 (b) 6 (c) 0.

An ace is the most dangerous card, since it is entirely possible that Joe has A-Q or A-A. Joe may have decided not to play it cagey by checking because you are getting pretty good odds to call. On the other hand, he may have decided that he is prepared to call with a lesser hand and is just trying to save himself £2000. Remember, from his viewpoint, one of your most likely hands is trip sevens.

Answer 8: (a) 10 (b) 2 (c) 4 (d) 7.

Joe may be trapping you. On the other hand, by going all-in, you are not risking facing a reraise. Making a small 'gay' bet in order to encourage a call with a poor hand seems terribly dangerous. It depends on your attitude to risk and your reading of Joe. Is he a fool, who must be parted from his money as quickly as possible, before others lay their greedy hands on it? Is he a rock who is just encouraging you to impale yourself on his trip queens? Does he look disappointed by the river card? In that case, if he is genuine, there is little point in betting. On the other hand, if he is moodying (play-acting), don't give him the satisfaction of losing even more money to him.

Hand 3

Getting one's just Desserts?

INTRODUCTION

Way back in 1979 I was playing seven-card stud at the Silverbird Hotel in Las Vegas. I wasn't doing particularly well and, after dinner, I decided to take a wander downtown. There were several pot-limit hold'em games in progress, a game of which I had little experience at that time. I asked the poker host to direct me to the smallest game and soon afterwards was settled in a $1-$2 blinds game.

I held 10♦-7♦ in fifth position. Seat 3 raised to $5 and seat 4 called. Thus the pot was $13 and it was $5 to call.

THE PLAY

Question 1: Should I: (a) pass (b) call (c) raise $5 (d) raise $18?

(a) ☐	(b) ☐	(c) ☐	(d) ☐	Points: ....

Action: Of course, I called. (To tell the truth, I am not even sure that my magnificent holding was suited!) Players 6 and 7 called. Now the player on the button raised $33, both blinds passed and seats 3 and 4 both called. Thus the pot was $132.

Question 2: Should I: (a) pass (b) call (c) raise $33 (d) raise $165?

(a) ☐	(b) ☐	(c) ☐	(d) ☐	Points: ....

Action: I called and seats 6 and 7 also called. This is more like a limit game than pot-limit. Even then, there is no justification for playing with such rubbish.

Flop: 10♥-7♠-6♣. I held 10♦-7♦. The pot was $231.

Action: Seat 3 went all-in for $200 and seat 4 raised a further $200 all-in. The pot stood at $831.

Question 3: Should I: (a) pass (b) call (c) raise $400 all-in?

(a) ☐	(b) ☐	(c) ☐	Points: ....
			Total: ....

Action: I raised $400 and seats 6 and 7 both passed. The button now made the following little speech, 'Well, if he was playing properly, I must still be winning.' He called.

He turned over his miserable collection of A♣-J♣. I am used to playing as we do in England, with the last bettor showing his hand. I turned over my two pair.

Turn and River: 10♥-7♠-6♣-2♠-Q♣. I held 10♦-7♦.

Neither of the other two players made a claim on the pot and thus I won a $2431 pot to which I had contributed $838. I had made a total profit of $1593 on the hand. Of course, I did not ask to see the hands of the two other players. That is always a mistake, since it not only antagonises them, but also they might have made a mistake and actually been winning. I must admit that I have often wondered what they could possibly have held.

The player who had bundled his money in on A♣-J♣ continued to wax lyrical about how bad a player I was to stay for the flop. Nobody pointed out to him that he played like a raving lunatic after the flop!

Later that evening I commented mildly to the poker host that he had told me my game was very small. His reply, 'Well, so it was, until you sat down!'

SCORECHART

30 That should not have been too difficult and was David's score. Of course you would have won absolutely nothing.

20-29 Presumably you managed the second pass. Danny scored 25.

10-19 I scored 10.

0-9 Did you really keep on calling and then pass the winning hand on the flop, faced by a bet and raise? Well, so might I now. But the past is a foreign country.

ANSWERS AND ANALYSIS

Holding: 10♦-7♦.

Answer 1: (a) 10 (b) 0 (c) 0 (c) 0.

This hand is nothing. The probability of hitting anything good is remote. The proper place for this filth is the garbage can.

Answer 2: (a) 10 (b) 0 (c) 0 (d) 0.

Well, if you got this one wrong then you have missed the point of this book. It is not to predict what action I took, but what I *should* have done!

Flop: 10♥-7♠-6♣.

Answer 3: (a) 5 (b) 0 (c) 10.

It is quite possible that I am beaten, but there is absolutely no reason just to call. What could possibly happen now? Surely no-one would be calling after all that action. Passing would be much better than just calling, and raising should be even better.

Hand 4

You don't always make the Right Decision

INTRODUCTION

Here we again delve into the past to a game at the Rainbow Casino in Birmingham. It was an eight-player £100 buy-in game with blinds of £1-£2.

One player had called in third position. I was in fifth, so there were three more players to act after me, plus the two blinds. There was £5 in the pot and I held A♠-10♦.

THE PLAY

Question 1: Should I: (a) pass (b) call (c) raise £2 (d) raise £7?

(a) ☐	(b) ☐	(c) ☐	(d) ☐	Points: ....

Action: I called, and so did three players after me. The small blind called and the big blind checked. There was now £14 in the pot.

Flop: A♥-9♠-5♦. I held A♠-10♦. The three players in front of me all checked.

Question 2: Should I: (a) check (b) bet £5 (c) bet £14?

(a) ☐	(b) ☐	(c) ☐	(d) ☐	Points: ....

Action: I bet £10. The next two players passed, John called on the button and the three players in front of me all passed. The pot now stood at £34.

Turn: A♥-9♠-5♦-A♣. I held A♠-10♦.

Question 3: Should I: (a) check (b) bet £10 (c) bet £34?

(a) ☐	(b) ☐	(c) ☐	Points: ....

Action: I bet £20. As this is a midway house between £10 and £34, I will award myself six marks. This should be enough to entice him in if I am winning. John called and raised a further £70. He had £20 left and the pot was £144.

Question 4: Should I: (a) pass (b) call (c) raise £20?

(a) ☐	(b) ☐	(c) ☐	Points: ....
			Total: ....

Action: I raised £20 and John called. He held A-J, so I had only three outs.

River: A♥-9♠-5♦-A♣-10♥. I held A♠-10♦ and had made a full house.

My friend Frank Thompson commented to me afterwards how right David Sklansky was. The problem with A-10 is that you so often encounter an opponent with an ace and a better kicker. This practical demonstration was a really cheap lesson for me – I had made a profit of £132!

SCORECHART

40 I am pleased that you play better than I did 25 years ago. But don't let it happen again if we face each other head-to-head!

30-39 I scored 32. David did a bit better, 34.

20-29 You probably overvalued the hand. Danny managed only 22.

10-19 You definitely need to read on.

4-9 If you play, try to do so with other people's money.

ANSWERS AND ANALYSIS

Holding: A♠-10♦.

Answer 1: (a) 4 (b) 10 (c) 2 (d) 0.

I had just recently read *Hold'em Poker* by David Sklansky, a little classic in which the author explained why you should be deeply suspicious of A-10. His ranking of hold'em hands was for limit poker, whereas mine in *Starting out in Poker* seeks to cover all varieties. No matter, we agree that A-10 is nothing to write home about, since it is too frequently dominated by an ace with a better kicker. It is an extremely bad hand with which to escalate the pot in middle position.

Flop: A♥-9♠-5♦.

Answer 2: (a) 0 (b) 4 (c) 10.

Nobody seemed keen before the flop. If I check and someone else bets, then I will not know where I am. I prefer to bet and, if raised, take fresh stock of the situation.

Turn: A♥-9♠-5♦-A♣.

Answer 3: (a) 10 (b) 4 (c) 8.

I should be deeply suspicious by now. My opponent probably has an ace and, since my short-term memory was good in those days, David Sklansky's advice should be ringing in my eyes. David Moskovic asks, 'Doesn't the second ace make it less likely he has an ace?' That is quite right. If he holds 9-5, he would now be drawing dead. Of course, there is no chance that I could push him out if he held a small full house.

Answer 4: (a) 10 (b) 0 (c) 6.

This is a difficult decision. It very much depends on how I read my opponent. He was a complete stranger to me. Some people would raise here with an ace and any kicker, whereas others would be certain to have A-K, 9-9 or 5-5. If I am up against one of the last two hands, I am a bit worse than 5/1 underdog. One thing is certain: if I call, then I will have to call the £20 on the river anyhow. Thus I should, as so often, either pass or raise all-in.

Hand 5

The Royal Game

INTRODUCTION

I was chatting one day to T.J. Cloutier, the author of *Championship No-Limit and Pot-Limit Hold'em* and *Championship Omaha*, who has won an inordinate number of tournaments. He asked us what we thought the most difficult hold'em hand was to play. I hazarded a guess at a pair of queens (which is probably true for a one-table satellite), but he told us that it was by far and away a pair of kings. The next few hands feature that particular holding.

I was playing at the Rainbow Casino in Birmingham many moons ago. We were all very inexperienced. The game was ten-handed and the blinds were £1-£2. I usually started with £500 in this £100 buy-in game and on this occasion had built it up into £1500.

I was in the big blind and everyone at the table had called the £2, while the small blind had called for the additional £1. Who can blame him? I would put that £1 in with any holding. There was now £20 in the pot. I held K♠-K♦.

THE PLAY

Question 1: Should I: (a) check (b) raise £2 (c) raise £10 (d) raise £20?

(a) ☐	(b) ☐	(c) ☐	(d) ☐	Points: ....

Action: I raised £20. Dirk, to my immediate left, called £20 as did two other players. I had succeeded in thinning down the crowd.

Flop: Q♦-8♠-4♥. I held K♠-K♦. The pot stood at £100.

Question 2: Should I: (a) check (b) bet £20 (c) bet £100?

(a) ☐	(b) ☐	(c) ☐	Points: ....

Action: I bet £90. Dirk raised the maximum of £280 and the other players passed. There was £560 in the middle.

Question 3: Should I: (a) pass (b) call (c) raise £280 (d) raise £840?

(a) ☐	(b) ☐	(c) ☐	(d) ☐	Points: ....

Action: I called.

Turn: Q♦-8♠-4♥-6♣. I held K♠-K♦. The pot stood at £840.

Question 4: Should I: (a) check (b) bet £250 (c) bet £840?

(a) ☐	(b) ☐	(c) ☐	Points: ....

Action: I checked and Dirk bet £840. There was £1680 in the pot and I had £1110 left on the table.

Question 5: Should I: (a) pass (b) call (c) raise all-in?

(a) ☐	(b) ☐	(c) ☐	Points: ....

Action: I called, so the pot was now £2520.

River: Q♦-8♠-4♥-6♣-3♣. I held K♠-K♦.

Question 6: Should I: (a) check (b) bet £270 all-in?

(a) ☐	(b) ☐	Points: ....

Action: I checked and Dirk bet £270 all-in. The pot was £2790.

Question 7: Should I: (a) pass (b) call?

(a) ☐	(b) ☐	Points: ....
		Total: ....

Action: I called and Dirk showed down his Q♥-4♠ to win a £3060 pot.

What was the reason it was such a bad call on the turn, rather than raising all-in? Had the river brought an eight, then Dirk would know that he had been outdrawn. The minimum I could sensibly have would then be A-Q coupled with Q-8-8 from the board. He would have Q-4 coupled with Q-8-8.

Helping me to drown my sorrows later that evening, Frank Thompson ruminated on how Dirk could possibly have called, out of position, with such filth before the flop. I still play against Dirk and recently mentioned to him that I was writing about some of our youthful encounters. He said he didn't have a clue at the time and was always bluffing with anything. Well, that was not my experience of him, although he was a loose player. But it did ease a 25-year-old scar.

SCORECHART

70 Well done, you rotter!

60-69	A fine score. Danny and I scored 61, whereas David managed 65.
45-59	Perhaps you were not aggressive enough.
30-44	Not your greatest chapter (at least I hope not!).
4-29	This is worrying.

ANSWERS AND ANALYSIS

Holding: K♠-K♦.

Answer 1: (a) 0 (b) 2 (c) 5 (d) 10.

I have a premium hand and should charge my loose as a goose opponents a premium to stay in the pot. Nowadays a £10 raise might be an interesting idea (although the actual sum would be more like £200), but in those innocent days, nobody would have noticed the difference. Of course, I am out of position, but the value of the hand does count for something.

Flop: Q♦-8♠-4♥.

Answer 2: (a) 3 (b) 0 (c) 10.

This is about as an innocuous-looking flop as it is possible to get. The only likely possible hand that would be beating me is trips, since the idea of flat-calling with a pair of aces before the flop would have been extremely advanced back in those days. A check on my part with this flop would signal that I had a strong hand.

Answer 3: (a) 0 (b) 10 (c) 0 (d) 6.

This is most mysterious. What is Dirk playing at? Surely, if he had trips, he would just flat call? His most likely hand has to be A-Q, but there is no need to raise and precipitate an all-in coup. Still I felt uncomfortable. I would have been far happier with a flop of Q♦-9♠-4♥, since then he might well have J-10 in the hole and be a big underdog.

Turn: Q♦-8♠-4♥-6♣.

Answer 4: (a) 10 (b) 0 (c) 5.

If I show weakness, he may bet A-Q. By checking, I am giving him the choice of taking a free card with such a holding. But he only has five outs and might have called me anyway. If I remember correctly, at this point I was regretting that I had so much money on the table. However, that was because I was a big winner in the game.

Answer 5: (a) 10 (b) 1 (c) 5.

Mine is not to reason why. Dirk obviously thought he had me beaten, so I should trust him – it was time to pass. Certainly a call is the worst play.

River: Q♦-8♠-4♥-6♣-3♣.

Answer 6: (a) 10 (b) 7.

It doesn't really matter, but if Dirk has got himself in seriously over his head, a bet would allow him to pass. With a check, he still has bluffing rights and may avail himself of them – to my advantage.

Answer 7: (a) -4 (b) 10.

It is too late and I must make a crying call.

Hand 6

There is no need to strip naked!

INTRODUCTION

Now you take on Frank Thompson's hand, still at the Rainbow Casino in Birmingham in 1980. The blinds were £2-£4 and Frank held K♠-K♦ in seat 9.

Two people had called including Dirk in seat 5. The player in seat 6 now passed and seat 7 now called £4 and made an £18 raise. The player in seat 8 passed, so it was £22 to Frank and the pot was £36.

THE PLAY

Question 1: Should Frank: (a) pass (b) call (c) raise £22 (d) raise £58?

(a) ☐ (b) ☐ (c) ☐ (d) ☐ Points: ....

Action: Frank raised £58. Everyone passed to Dirk, who called £76 and raised the full £192. Seat 7 passed and it was now back on Frank. The pot was £384 and both he and Dirk had £700 left on the table.

Question 2: Should Frank: (a) pass (b) call (c) raise £192 (d) raise £508 all-in?

(a) ☐ (b) ☐ (c) ☐ (d) ☐ Points: ....

Hypothetical Question 3: What if you held a pair of aces? Should you: (a) pass (b) call (c) raise £192 (d) raise £508 all-in?

(a) ☐ (b) ☐ (c) ☐ (d) ☐ Points: ....

Action: Now Frank made a big mistake. He passed his hand. Well, that is fair enough. However, while doing so he turned his kings over. This was an ego trip to show that he could make a big laydown. I remember being startled at the time to learn that it is reasonable to throw away kings before the flop. Frank said, 'Well, since he knows how I play, he should only raise with pocket aces or kings.' At this point Dirk showed us his pair of queens. Presumably this was another ego trip, or perhaps he was trying to wind Frank up.

Question 4: Now that we know Dirk could be raising with Q-Q in this situation, did Frank play mathematically incorrectly: (a) yes (b) it is just a matter of taste (c) no (d) I don't know?

(a) ☐	(b) ☐	(c) ☐	(d) ☐	Points: ....

Question 5: What should Frank do in the early stages of a long pot-limit or no-limit tournament: (a) pass (b) call (c) raise all-in?

(a) ☐	(b) ☐	(c) ☐		Points: ....
				Total: ....

SCORECHART

50 Frank got the right answer to Question 4 for the wrong reason. But hey, this is poker, not a philosophy seminar.

40-49 Eminently sensible play. David scored 49.

30-39 I would have scored 36 at that time by raising all-in even in a tournament, but today I would pass. Danny scored 32.

15-29 You may have become confused by the marginal choices.

0-14 Please do not say that you would have passed a pair of aces in a cash game.

ANSWERS AND ANALYSIS

Holding: K♠-K♦.

Answer 1: (a) 0 (b) 4 (c) 2 (d) 10.

Frank has a premium hand and good position. He would be shirking his duty, or slowplaying the hand, if he were not to reraise.

Answer 2: (a) 10 (b) 1 (c) 1 (d) 7.

Dirk has come on strong by making the third raise, but he has shown even more strength by check-raising. There is no shame in passing, but there is no great honour either. However, you want the cash, not the credit. A call or a small raise suggests very strongly that you have pocket kings. You do not want to send a telegram announcing your position.

Answer 3: (a) -5 (b) 10 (c) 4 (d) 9.

You are trying to trap Dirk for all his money and may well succeed if he has pocket kings. It is conceivable that you can still outplay Dirk on the flop if he too has pocket aces. However, this is unlikely to be his hand and it is even more unlikely that he will do you the honour of passing. Since there is always the chance of being outdrawn, it makes very good sense to raise and be done with it, although you are wasting your positional advantage.

Answer 4: (a) 0 (b) 8 (c) 10 (d) 0.

Well, I do know – it is much more likely that Dirk has either aces or queens. We don't know whether he would also raise with A-K suited, but he will pass Q-Q or A-K if you reraise, and will probably also pass K-K. Thus, should you raise and get a call, you are going to be up against aces, which you will occasionally outdraw. It is a very close decision.

How did I work that out? Well, I will explain the maths here. Do not bother to look unless you are seriously masochistic or arithmetically obsessed.

WARNING: Complex maths follows

There are six combinations for Dirk to have a pair of aces. Similarly there are six ways for him to have a pair of queens. There is only one combination for the other two kings. Thus there are 13 hands and we should consider the outcome if the hand were to be played out 13 times.

Frank calls £192 and raises £508 every time. Thus he is risking £700 x 13 = £9100.

The pot is always £1084 before Dirk decides about his £508.

Six times he has queens and passes. Return to Frank = £6504

Once he has kings and passes. Return to Frank = £1084

Six times he has aces and calls, after which Frank will outdraw Dirk 18.1% of the time*. Return to Frank = £1177

Total return for Frank if Dirk has A-A, K-K or Q-Q = **£8765**

Thus you lose less than 4% if you raise all-in. It is not a mistake to raise, but nor is it a mistake to pass. If Dirk could be conceivably be playing with A-K suited, then it is a definite raise.

There is no conceivable reason that you should ever want to make such calculations at the table. It is sufficient to remember you had better watch out if ever you are facing a bet and two raises in one round of betting in any poker game.

*It is well-known that the underpair is 9/2 underdog before the flop.

Answer 5: (a) 10 (b) 0 (c) 0.

Clearly the decision is extremely marginal, but you are out of the tournament if you get it wrong. That is a completely different scenario from having to dig up more money from your pocket. If you pass, £700 is clearly enough with which to play sensible poker in that particular tournament.

Hand 7

Risk Assessment

INTRODUCTION

This was my last-ever tournament in the World Series of Poker at Binion's Horseshoe in Las Vegas in 2001. It was a two-day no-limit tournament with, I think, a $3000 buy-in. I have adjusted the hand to the pot-limit structure.

I held K♠-K♦ in seventh position. It was early on the first day and the blinds were $100-$200. Ali, whom you may have met in the Omaha book, was first after the blinds and made it $600 to go. This is known as an 'O'Neil' bet (he could have made it $800). Two players had called, so the pot stood at $2100 and it was $600 to me.

THE PLAY

Question 1: Should I: (a) pass (b) call (c) raise $600 (d) raise $2700?

(a) ☐	(b) ☐	(c) ☐	(d) ☐	Points: ....

Action: I raised $2700 and everyone passed to Ali, who reraised $8100. The players between us passed. Ali had an additional $1000 left and I had $9100.

Question 2: Should I: (a) pass (b) call $8100 (c) raise $1000 all-in.

(a) ☐	(b) ☐	(c) ☐	Points: ....

Action: I raised $1000 all-in. There was $26,300 in the pot.

Flop, Turn and River: Q♥-9♥-2♥-Q♠-8♣. I held K♠-K♦. Ali held K♥-K♣.

Phew! Thus I got away from the hand and split the pot. Before the flop was turned over, our cards were put on their backs, as is the custom in tournaments.

Question 3: What action would we have taken in a cash game: (a) none, just let the cards be dealt (b) agreed to save $5000 (c) split the money (d) dealt the cards out twice?

(a) ☐	(b) ☐	(c) ☐	(d) ☐	Points: ....
				Total: ....

SCORECHART

30 Well done indeed.

20-29 I scored 28. David and Danny only managed 20, but they are unused to making deals.

10-19 A rather poor score

0-9 I'll come out of hold'em retirement to play in your game.

ANSWERS AND ANALYSIS

Holding: K♠-K♦.

Answer 1: (a) 0 (b) 2 (c) 4 (d) 10.

Of course, you will recognise elements of the situation from the last two hands. I do not know what effect a gay raise of $600 would have had. A pot raise is in order.

Answer 2: (a) 10 (b) 0 (c) 8.

I am risking my entire stack when I have adequate funds left to play serious poker. Ali was not fooling around; he clearly had a strong hand.

However, my reasoning was somewhat different. If Ali held pocket aces, surely he would not have made that gay raise when first to speak. This would only have served to alert the table to the fact that he had a good hand. Thus he did not have aces and I could not be losing.

Answer 3: (a) 0 (b) 2 (c) 10 (d) 3.

It is just a crapshoot, neither player has any advantage. Theoretically such a split would not be allowed in London, but frankly that is just silly. We would never be permitted to chop the pot in a tournament.

WARNING: Complex maths follows

Of course, the other players were licking their lips. As you can see from the flop, there were three hearts. Ali had a 36% chance of knocking me out. In a tournament, every player knocked out is a step in the right direction for the remaining players.

Had Ali and I known the situation before any action had occurred, we should both have passed! We split $1500, thus receiving $750 profit each, for which we risked $12,400 each and the chance of being knocked out of the tournament. This would happen to each of us only 2.2% of the time, which is perfectly good odds in a money game, but a poor risk in a tournament.

Had I passed Ali's reraise, I would have lost $3300 instead of winning $750. That is too much equity for me to pass because of a 50/1 shot.

Note that since Ali was first to speak and thus able to make the last big raise, it was he who had the advantage. The initiative often outweighs the advantage of acting last in such positions.

What do you think of Ali's O'Neil raise to $600? It seems to me it was rather clever. Had another player raised after I had done so, Ali would have been able to pass his kings without compunction and at a cost of only $600 in the hand.

Hand 8

Plugging the Gap

♣ – ♥ – ♦ – ♠ – ♣ – ♥ – ♦ – ♠

INTRODUCTION

Early days again. We were in Birmingham and the blinds were £1-£2, a £100 game.

I held J♣-10♣ in seat 5. Robert, first after the blinds, raised to £5. Number 4 called. Thus there was £13 in the pot.

THE PLAY

Question 1: Should I: (a) pass (b) call (c) raise £5 (d) raise £18?

(a) ☐	(b) ☐	(c) ☐	(d) ☐	Points: ....

Action: I called, as did seat 6. Roy then raised the pot £28 from seat 8. Seat 9 called and everyone else passed until it reached Robert, who called with £300 remaining in front of him. Seat 4 now folded and the pot stood at £117.

Question 2: Should I: (a) pass (b) call (c) raise £28 (c) raise £145?

(a) ☐	(b) ☐	(c) ☐	Points: ....

Action: I called and seat 6 passed. The pot stood at £145.

Flop: A♣-10♦-5♣. I held J♣-10♣. Robert bet the full £145 and the pot was now £290.

Question 3: Should I: (a) pass (b) call (c) raise £100 (d) raise £435?

(a) ☐	(b) ☐	(c) ☐	(d) ☐	Points: ....

Action: I called, Roy raised £500, seat 9 passed and Robert called £155 all-in. The main pot stood at £890 and Roy had created a side pot of £345.

Hypothetical Question 4: If it was all-in for £500, should I: (a) pass (b) call?

(a) ☐	(b) ☐	Points: ....

In reality, Roy had £2000 left.

Question 5: Should I: (a) pass (b) call (c) raise £500 (d) raise £1700?

(a) ☐ (b) ☐ (c) ☐ (d) ☐ Points: ....

Hypothetical Question 6: What if I have read it all wrong, and in fact Roy has K♣-Q♣ and Robert a pair of nines? Approximately what percentage of the side pot would I then win: (a) 40% (b) 45% (c) 50% (d) 55% (e) 60%?

(a) ☐ (b) ☐ (c) ☐ (d) ☐ (e) ☐ Points: ....

Action: I called. Well, wouldn't you with only about three month's experience?

Turn: A♣-10♦-5♣-6♣. I held J♣-10♣. The pot stood at £1735 and Roy had £2000 left.

Question 7: Should I: (a) check (b) bet £500 (c) bet £1700?

(a) ☐ (b) ☐ (c) ☐ Points: ....

Action: I bet £1600. I knew this was a little less than the pot, but I often do this. It spreads seeds of doubt in player's minds. What if I held 10♥-10♣? Then I might be trying to push out trip aces (if this is what Roy has).

Hypothetical Question 8: Taking over Roy's hand. (You have to forget that you know precisely what I held!) I can reveal that he held A♠-A♥. He faced a £1600 bet for a pot of £3335. Should he: (a) pass (b) call (c) raise £400 all-in?

(a) ☐ (b) ☐ (c) ☐ Points: ....

Action: Roy called.

River: A♣-10♦-5♣-6♣-6♥. I held J♣-10♣. The pot stood at £4935.

Question 9: Should I: (a) check (b) bet £400? Remember you must forget that you know about Roy's actual hand!

(a) ☐ (b) ☐ Points: ....

Action: I checked and he bet £400. The pot was £5335.

Question 10: Should I: (a) pass (b) call £400?

(a) ☐ (b) ☐ Points: ....

Total: ....

Action: I called and of course he won with A-A for aces full. Robert showed us his own ace, so I was quite right; Roy had only eight wins with nine cards accounted for. Thus he was (43-8)/8 or nearly 9/2 against filling up.

As Roy was scooping in the money, he said, 'I would have been disappointed not to have won that pot.' Well, so indeed was I.

SCORECHART

100 Wow, that's good.

85-100 I scored 92, while David made 87 and Danny 86. Well, they didn't have the advantage of playing the hand or writing the quiz!

70-84 Perhaps you lost concentration at some point?

50-69 A hand you could play too loosely or too tight or both.

30-49 To win money at poker, you need to make more than 50% of the correct decisions.

15-29 Better luck next time.

3-14 The next hand is much simpler.

ANSWERS AND ANALYSIS

Holding: J♣-10♣.

Answer 1: (a) 7 (b) 10 (c) 0 (d) 0.

Mine is a marginal hand and I was in middle position. Most people will take on this hand for such a small sum.

Answer 2: (a) 10 (b) 8 (c) -2 (d) -5.

I have been whip-lashed. That is, first raised from my right and then from my left. My hand is now purely a drawing one and I am out of position. I certainly do not have huge implied odds. However, I was getting 4/1 for my money, so my call is based virtually entirely on actual pot odds.

What are the odds of my hitting the flop and then my hand standing up? I would not know how to go about making that calculation. Many people make the mistake of thinking that all you have to do is run hands through a computer and look at the percentages at the end of the pot. This is completely fallacious. Often you would win by a backdoor outdraw. For instance, in this hand it may come K-3-2 on the flop. I would not consider calling, but when the hand concludes K-3-2-Q-9 I have made the nut straight and am now 'Lord of all I see'.

Flop: A♣-10♦-5♣.

Answer 3: (a) -1 (b) 10 (c) 0 (d) 5.

I was so inexperienced at the time that I think this was the first time I had ever met this particular constellation. It is variation of 'Morton's fork'. Either

I am beating Robert or have the best draw. Passing would be stupid and raising is not a good idea, since there are two players to act after me.

Answer 4: (a) 0 (b) 10.

I would have adequate odds for my money.

Answer 5: (a) 10 (b) 4 (c) 0 (d) 3.

I have been whip-lashed for the second time in the same hand. Can I still be in a 'Morton's fork' situation? I think not. Roy made the second raise before the flop, and has done the same again when he could be certain that Robert would call (since Robert would not be stupid enough to bet £145 and then pass for another £155). Roy must have a made hand.

I can win £1235 for my £500. However, if the turn brings a blank then I am going to have to face another bet.

Answer 6: (a) 5 (b) 10 (c) 6 (d) 4 (e) 0.

That is the way it is. I am an underdog, even if I have the best made hand.

Okay, so I do not have adequate pot odds to call. What about if I hit my flush on the turn? Surely I can bet and win a substantial sum? I must have adequate implied odds here? That is true, but Roy will only call, if at all, with a set of aces and then I can still be outdrawn. No, it is a clear pass.

Turn: A♣-10♦-5♣-6♣.

Answer 7: (a) 4 (b) 3 (c) 10.

I have hit my hand. I could try a check in the hope of a bet from a losing hand, but the only hand that might try such a bet is A-A and it is quite likely that Roy will call anyway if that is his holding. Roy is going to pass any hand other than pocket aces or the dreaded K♣-Q♣.

Answer 8: (a) 10 (b) 0 (c) 4.

WARNING: Complex maths follows

Trip aces are very nice, but they are almost certainly losing here, unless you can bring yourself to believe that I was playing 10♥-10♣ in such a sophisticated manner. There are at most ten cards left with which you can improve. You can see your two cards and the four belonging to the turn. This leaves 46 unseen. The odds against your making the hand is (46-10)/10, which makes it roughly 7/2 against your winning. In fact, it is quite likely that Robert has an ace in his hand, which would make it 4/1 against.

If you do call, will you really have the bottle to pass on the river for just £400 in a pot of £5335? Of course not! Thus you may as well raise all-in.

Once Roy calls, my implied odds have worked out. At this point I am winning £1235 plus £1600 for my risk of calling Roy's £500 raise on the flop. We can also add in the £400 that Roy is going to call on the river, which comes to £3235 for £500. This comes to around 13/2 – and I was only 4/1 against making the flush on the turn! But as you will see, this is too simplistic.

River: A♣-10♦-5♣-6♣-6♥.

Where did my beloved implied odds go? Just because I have been outdrawn does not mean that I have played incorrectly.

My profit is £3235, but my hand only stands up 80% of the time. Profit £2588.

I am risking a further £2000 and 20% of the time I lose. Loss £400.

Thus my total expected profit is £2188 for a cost of £500, which is just slightly better than my 4/1 odds for hitting the flush. However, there are some imponderables here. Robert could have had K♣-Q♣, when I am drawing dead to the main pot. Roy could (and should) pass if he is staring at a possible flush on the turn.

Answer 9: (a) 10 (b) 4.

It is conceivable that I am winning. If so, he is unlikely to call £400, but he might try to bluff it.

Answer 10: (a) 2 (b) 10.

This is for so little money in such a big pot that you must make a crying call. There is a hand later in the book where I passed for even less money, but the situation was different.

Hand 9

My Friends clash

INTRODUCTION

This hand took place in 1980 in a small tournament at the Victoria Casino in London, now the Grosvenor Victoria. To tell the truth, it was in a small no-limit tournament, but I have adjusted the game to pot-limit. I only know about the hand because Frank Thompson explained it to me some months later.

The blinds were £200-£400. Everyone had passed around to Corky who was the small blind. He called for £200 and there was therefore £800 in the pot. Corky and Frank each had £1300 left in chips. (By the way, you may have met my friend Corky on page 62 of *Starting out in Poker*.) Frank, in the big blind held K♠-?. That is right, he had only looked at one card.

THE PLAY

Question 1: Should he: (a) check (b) bet £200 (c) bet £800 (d) look at his second card and then make a decision?

(a) ☐	(b) ☐	(c) ☐	(d) ☐	Points: ....

Action: Frank raised £800 and Corky raised £500 all-in for both players. The pot stood at £2900.

Question 2: Should Frank: (a) pass (b) call (c) look at his second card and then make a decision?

(a) ☐	(b) ☐	(c) ☐	Points: ....
			Total: ....

Action: Frank called. It turned out that he had K♠-8♦. Corky had Q♦-Q♣. The pair of queens stood up and so did Frank, as he was out of the tournament.

SCORECHART

20 I do hope that you achieved the maximum score, as did Danny.

10-19 Frank (now a seasoned veteran professional) and David only scored 10. Well, Frank might resent being called a veteran!

0-9 That takes some doing!

ANSWERS AND ANALYSIS

Holding: K♠-?.

Answer 1: (a) 0 (b) 0 (c) 0 (d) 10.

WARNING: Complex maths follows

It cost Corky £200 to call the big blind. There is £600 in the pot, so Corky can pass the bottom 25% of his possible hands. He should raise with the top 50%, without considering a bluff. Taking a 10% chance of a bluff into account, the range of calling hands is a negligible 15% (whichever hands that may mean). Thus Corky should have raised or passed. Calling was irrational and Frank should have been very wary indeed. He should look at his hand and perhaps only raise with A-A, K-K or A-K. Whenever your opponent makes what looks like a senseless play, warning bells should go off in your head.

Answer 2: (a) -5 (b) 10 (c) 5.

Frank does not have enough money to pass this hand. He is getting nearly 6/1 for his chips, so must call and hope to win. I will award you full marks if you intended to look first, but only if you were going to call no matter what.

Hand 10

Alone Together

INTRODUCTION

This hand was played in the seniors' tournament in the 2001 World Series of Poker in Las Vegas. It was actually played no-limit, but in this case that made little difference to how the pot was played.

I held A♦-6♣. We had started with $1000 in chips and it was still early in the tournament. My stack was now $1100, since I had managed to win one small pot. Each of these tournaments is held over two days, but clearly the organisers did not want to risk very long sessions, since the blinds were $25-$50.

I was in the small blind and everyone had passed around to me. Only Ben was left to conquer. From what little I knew of him, he seemed to be a good, solid player.

THE PLAY

Question 1: Should I: (a) pass (b) call (c) raise $50 (d) raise $100?

(a) ☐	(b) ☐	(c) ☐	(d) ☐	Points: ....

Action: I called. I, too, wonder why. Perhaps it was a momentary lack of concentration?

Hypothetical Action: What if I had played correctly and raised $100, but then Ben had raised a further $300?

Question 2: Should I: (a) pass (b) call (c) raise $300 (d) raise $650 all-in?

(a) ☐	(b) ☐	(c) ☐	(d) ☐	Points: ....

Action: In the actual hand Ben checked it back at me. We had reached the flop without incident.

Flop: A♥-8♦-6♠. I held A♦-6♣. Well, that was nice! The pot was $100 and I had $1050 left in the tank.

Question 3: Should I: (a) check (b) bet $50 (c) bet $100?

(a) ☐	(b) ☐	(c) ☐	Points: ....

Action: I checked and Ben bet $75. The pot stood at $175.

Question 4: Should I: (a) pass (b) call (c) raise $75 (d) raise $250?

(a) ☐	(b) ☐	(c) ☐	(d) ☐	Points: ....

Action: I raised $200. Note, my deliberate shaving of the amount. This may suggest to Ben that I am prepared to pass a reraise. Ben now raised the pot $650. I had $775 left and there was $1300 in the pot.

Question 5: Should I: (a) pass (b) call (c) raise $125 all-in?

(a) ☐	(b) ☐	(c) ☐	Points: ....

Action: I raised $125 and Ben called. The pot stood at $2200.

As we turned our hands over, Ben said to me, 'You're winning.' The next moment came the turn and he said, 'But I've outdrawn you.'

Turn and River: A♥-8♦-6♠-8♠-3♦. I held A♦-6♣ and Ben held A♠-Q♦.

Thus Ben won with A♠-Q♦-A♥-8♦-8♠ against my A♦-6♣-A♥-8♦-8♠. That was the end of my challenge in this event. Of course, it is better to be out early, rather than to finish one off the money.

Why didn't Ben raise before the flop? His hand isn't good enough to slowplay. Perhaps he was deeply suspicious of me as per the previous hand. But, in that case, he should pass my raise on the flop. Anyway, it probably would have made no difference. I would have called and the pot would still have proceeded as above, but quicker.

My only way of escaping was to raise before the flop. In that case Ben might well have reraised and I could then have passed.

However, the fact is that I managed to engineer an all-in situation where I was a substantial favourite. You are not going to win tournaments by waiting for the absolute nuts.

Question 6: Approximately what percentage of the hands do I win from the flop?

(a) 50% (b) 61% (c) 73% (d) 81%?

(a) ☐	(b) ☐	(c) ☐	(d) ☐	Points: ....

Hypothetical Action: Instead of reraising, Ben just calls my check-raise on the flop. This, in my opinion was the better play for him. He has position and it is a 'Morton's fork' situation. If he is losing, he may be able to get away from the hand, whereas if he is winning, he may win more. One thing seems clear: if he is winning, I will almost certainly pass a reraise.

Hypothetical Turn is the same: A♥-8♦-6♠-8♠. I held A♦-6♣. The pot stands at $650.

Hypothetical Question 7: Should I: (a) check (b) bet $200 (c) bet $650?

(a) ☐	(b) ☐	(c) ☐	Points: ....

Hypothetical Action: I check and so does Ben.

Hypothetical River: A♥-8♦-6♠-8♠-3♦. I held A♦-6♣. The pot is $650.

Question 8: Should I: (a) check (b) bet $200 (c) bet $650?

(a) ☐	(b) ☐	(c) ☐	Points: ....

Hypothetical Action: I check and Ben bets $500.

Question 9: Should I: (a) pass (b) call (c) raise $275 all-in?

(a) ☐	(b) ☐	(c) ☐	Points: ....
			Total: ....

SCORECHART

90 Perfect play, find a game other than mine.

80-89 I scored 82.

65-79 David and Danny both scored 71. Highly acceptable.

50-64 You will quickly find yourself out of chips in tournaments.

30-49 Only play in tournaments with very small buy-ins.

0-29 You still have a great deal of work to do on your technique.

ANSWERS AND ANALYSIS

Holding: A♦-6♣.

Answer 1: (a) 0 (b) 2 (c) 4 (d) 10.

Two-handed this is strong favourite to be beating whatever Ben has. It is probably best to raise the maximum. Otherwise Ben, who had far more chips than me, might take it into his head to reraise and try to take me off the hand. Then I would not know where I stood. An investment of $125 is a high percentage of my mediocre stack to devote to this cause, but what can you do? It is as good a situation as any.

Answer 2: (a) 10 (b) 4 (c) -1 (d) 2.

This is not much of a hand to go to war with. I knew little about Ben, and would have no reason to believe that he was simply trying to steal the pot. After all, he had only $2000 in front of him. There is no reason for him to risk a substantial dent in his stack so early in the game.

Flop: A♥-8♦-6♠.

Answer 3: (a) 10 (b) 0 (c) 4.

I should usually slowplay such a hand. Ben probably has nothing and will check right back, but then I can bet the turn and he may well try to steal the pot off me.

Answer 4: (a) -5 (b) 5 (c) 3 (d) 10.

There is nothing wrong with slowplaying the hand by calling. However, I need to amass some chips. Making a gay raise does not fill the bill here. Of course, Ben could have a range of hands from absolutely nothing to a set of aces!

Answer 5: (a) 0 (b) 2 (c) 10.

It is extremely unlikely that Ben is raising with trips. Why be so pushy when he has position? Thus the only hand I have to fear is A-8 and he would probably have slowplayed that as well. He could even have 9-7. There is no point at all in just calling.

Answer 6: (a) 0 (b) 5 (c) 10 (d) 5.

Possibly, like me, you thought that my hand was an even bigger favourite. Ben has six outs on the turn and nine with one card to come if the turn card is higher than a six. Of course, I may hit a full house.

Answer 7: (a) 10 (b) 0 (c) 0.

Logic tells us that he most probably has an ace. He will therefore be winning with any kicker above a six. He will be behind with any card below a six, but unbeknownst to him, will have a very good chance of splitting the pot. In this case any card seven or higher results in a split as my six would then not play.

Answer 8: (a) 10 (b) 0 (c) 2.

I am not going to be called unless I am losing. I should not use up nearly all my chips tilting at a windmill where I am almost certainly losing and am going to be called.

Answer 9: (a) 10 (b) 2 (c) 0.

Of course, we know that Ben is winning. But it seems obvious to me that he has the better hand, except when he may be bluffing with 9-7.

Hand 11

Poker can be very frustrating

INTRODUCTION

This was another no-limit hold'em tournament in Vegas. However, again the hand played just like pot-limit and I have made the appropriate adjustments.

It was $3000 buy-in with blinds at this stage of $100-$200. Jack Keller, a former winner of the World Series of Poker Championship, was in the big blind with 5♣-4♠. He had $15,000 in chips, having made quite good progress in the tournament. You are following his hand.

Three people had called the big blind of $200 including Devilfish (less well-known by his real name, Dave Ulliott) who had $20,000 in chips. The small blind made it up to $200, so the pot stood at $1000.

THE PLAY

Question 1: Should Jack: (a) check (b) raise $200 (c) raise $1000?

(a) ☐	(b) ☐	(c) ☐	Points: ....

Action: Jack checked.

Flop: 5♥-5♦-4♣. Jack held 5♣-4♠. The pot was $1000 and the small blind checked.

Question 2: Should Jack: (a) check (b) bet $200 (c) bet $1000?

(a) ☐	(b) ☐	(c) ☐	Points: ....

Action: Jack checked, the next two players checked and Devilfish bet $1000. The small blind now passed and the pot stood at $2000.

Question 3: Should Jack: (a) pass (b) call (c) raise $1000 (d) raise $3000?

(a) ☐	(b) ☐	(c) ☐	(d) ☐	Points: ....

Action: Jack called $1000 and the other two players passed. The pot stood at $3000.

Turn: 5♥-5♦-4♣-6♠. Jack held 5♣-4♠.

Question 4: Should Jack: (a) check (b) bet $1000 (c) bet $3000?

(a) ☐	(b) ☐	(c) ☐	Points: ....

Action: Jack checked and Devilfish bet $3000. The pot stood at $6000 and Jack had $14,000 left in chips.

Question 5: Should Jack: (a) pass (b) call (c) raise $3000 (d) raise $9000?

(a) ☐	(b) ☐	(c) ☐	(d) ☐	Points: ....

Action: Jack raised $9000 and Devilfish reraised $2000 all-in. The pot was $29,000.

Question 6: Should Jack: (a) pass (b) call?

(a) ☐	(b) ☐	Points: ....
		Total: ....

Action: Jack called and Devilfish revealed 6-6. He thus won the pot with sixes full and Jack was out of the tournament.

Jack subsequently joined our side-action table. He told me the whole gory story and then complained bitterly that he would not have been involved, except that he was on the big blind and there was no raise before the flop.

Of course Devilfish got lucky, but he played the pot perfectly. It is seldom a good idea to raise with a small pair before the flop. It was not unreasonable to assume that his pocket sixes were probably winning on the flop, after all, everyone else has checked. He did not slowplay his nut full house on the turn and got the lot.

SCORECHART

60 Like Jack, David and I, you would have made the maximum score and lost the maximum amount. Sometimes it happens in poker that you play perfectly, run into a brick wall and lose. However, you should not allow yourself to go on tilt.

50-59 A good score. Perhaps you realised that you were being set up and played accordingly. Danny made 50.

35-49 Well, you are safe behind the pages of a book.

20-34 This really is not good enough to become a money player.

0-19 You should not be let out by yourself.

♣ – ♥ – ♦ – ♠ – ♣ – ♥ – ♦ – ♠

ANSWERS AND ANALYSIS

Holding: 5♣-4♠.

Answer 1: (a) 10 (b) -1 (c) -2.

This is a very mediocre hand, but it is possible to hit a good flop. No hand is ever worthless at poker, provided you have a freeroll.

Flop: 5♥-5♦-4♣.

Answer 2: (a) 10 (b) -1 (c) 0.

This is not a hand to get too excited about. It is unlikely that Jack is going to win very much here, since he is just too strong.

Answer 3: (a) -5 (b) 10 (c) 0 (d) 0.

There will never be a better time to slowplay a hand. Two players are still to come and may conceivably take action. Devilfish does not need much encouragement to try to steal a pot. He may have nothing, or perhaps 7-6. This game is not like pot-limit Omaha, where you should generally raise in this kind of situation, since it is too easy for your opponents to hit an overpair.

Turn: 5♥-5♦-4♣-6♠.

Answer 4: (a) 10 (b) 3 (c) 0.

We can reasonably assume that Devilfish may have another go at this pot, even with nothing. If not, well, no harm done, since with nothing he would not call a bet anyway.

Answer 5: (a) -5 (b) 5 (c) 0 (d) 10.

If Jack plays passively and checks, then Devilfish will smell a rat and pass on the river, unless he hits his overpair. Thus a full-blooded raise is in order.

Answer 6: (a) 0 (b) 10.

It is looking ominous, but Devilfish could have the same hand or be raising on A-5. Anyway, the pot is too big now to think about it.

Hand 12

Just one of those Things

INTRODUCTION

This hand occurred in a £1000 game at the Grosvenor Victoria Casino in London some years ago. The blinds were £25-£25.

I held A♣-J♣ in fifth position. Nobody had called after the two blinds and there were four players left to act, one of whom was Colm, a rock-solid player, and the other, Brian, who was always prepared to escalate the pot.

THE PLAY

Question 1: Should I: (a) pass (b) call (c) raise £25 (d) raise £75?

(a) ☐	(b) ☐	(c) ☐	(d) ☐	Points: ....

Action: I called, as did Colm. Brian lived up to expectations and raised £100. The other players passed around to me and the pot stood at £225.

Question 2: Should I: (a) pass (b) call (c) raise £100 (d) raise £325?

(a) ☐	(b) ☐	(c) ☐	(d) ☐	Points: ....

Action: I raised £300 and both Colm and Brian called.

Flop: J♠-J♦-3♣. I held A♣-J♣. The pot was £1325.

Question 3: Should I: (a) check (b) bet £300 (c) bet £1300?

(a) ☐	(b) ☐	(c) ☐	Points: ....

Action: I checked and surprise, surprise so did Colm. Brian bet £1300.

Question 4: Should I: (a) pass (b) call (c) raise £1300 (d) raise £3900?

(a) ☐	(b) ☐	(c) ☐	(d) ☐	Points: ....

Action: I raised £3000 and Colm reraised all-in £3000. Exit Brian, presumably pursuing his own demons. The pot stood at £14,225.

Question 5: Should I: (a) pass (b) call?

(a) ☐	(b) ☐	Points: ....
		Total: ....

Action: I called. Colm showed down a full house threes, which stood up.

Ouch! What can you do? It was equally likely that he held A-J as 3-3. He would need one of three aces and the case jack for the former, and two of the three remaining treys for the latter. Also, it was just possible Colm had opened up and I was winning against K-J or Q-J.

In any case, A-J wins the pot here almost 23% of the time against 3-3, a bit worse than 3/1. If that is his holding, I would get back almost £3800 for a £3000 call on the average.

Poker can be very frustrating. It was infuriating to lose my biggest pot of the night against the tightest player! That is one disadvantage of playing against extremely loose, aggressive opponents: they can march you into ferocious storms.

David asked me whether Colm played badly pre-flop. He won about £9000 for his £400 call before the flop, which seems marginal to me. Brian could also have raised again after Colm had called my reraise. Unquestionably, in the early stages of a tournament, this would have been bad play. The 'law of conservation of chips' requires that you do not fritter away chips with a mediocre holding.

SCORECHART

50 Well done. And like me, you would have got well done!

40-49 Perhaps you acted too soon. Don't tell me you passed at the end with such good odds? David scored 40.

25-39 You need to improve your poker skills.

10-24 Danny scored 23. An utterly miserable result.

0-9 Poker 'skills' is not exactly the right term.

ANSWERS AND ANALYSIS

Holding: A♣-J♣.

Answer 1: (a) 0 (b) 10 (c) 2 (d) 5.

I count this as the seventh best hold'em hand. It is worth a raise, but why bother here when Brian is likely to make the running? Perhaps he will raise and someone else will reraise, leaving me with a decision, but having spent only £25 so far.

Answer 2: (a) -5 (b) 3 (c) 5 (d) 10.

If you decide to pass, having called with this type of player still to act, you need your head examined. Calling before he acts in such circumstances, is just a waste of money. All I have learned so far is that Colm is willing to call a raise from Brian. He is much too wily a player not to have noticed the pattern as I had done. He may have a better hand than me – and of course this is also true of Brian. However, the force is with me at the moment.

Flop: J♠-J♦-3♣.

Answer 3: (a) 10 (b) 0 (c) 0.

A leopard does not change its spots. Brian must be given an opportunity to bet.

Answer 4: (a) -5 (b) 5 (c) 7 (d) 10.

Of course, I have an exceptional hand, and there are various ways of playing it. Brian was not given to continuing a bluff if anyone showed opposition. Thus totally slowplaying the hand is not necessarily the best course of action. I had discounted Colm as a likely contender.

Answer 5: (a) 0 (b) 10.

The worst he can have from my point of view is J-3, and even then I might outdraw him. Anyway, I would fall off my chair if Colm really held J-3. It is much more likely that he has A-J, splitting the pot, or 3-3.

Hand 13

A Bad Beat Story

INTRODUCTION

I have been playing poker with David Levy since 1964. In 1980 his company Intelligent Games commissioned me to prepare material for computers to play poker. I guess we were the pioneers in the field. We had created software for the machine to play hold'em, and David came in to try it out for himself. He had never played hold'em before. The blinds were a notional \$1-\$2 and David was in the small blind with Q♦-10♦. The pot was \$3.

THE PLAY

Question 1: Should David: (a) pass (b) call (c) raise \$1 (d) raise \$4?

(a) ☐	(b) ☐	(c) ☐	(d) ☐	Points: ....

Action: We did not want the machine to pass, so David just called.

Flop: A♦-K♦-J♦. David held Q♦-10♦. The programmer and I laughed and explained to David what had happened. The pot was \$4.

Question 2: Should David: (a) check (b) bet \$1 (c) bet \$4?

(a) ☐	(b) ☐	(c) ☐	Points: ....

Action: David checked, as did the machine.

Turn: A♦-K♦-J♦-4♥. David held Q♦-10♦.

Question 3: Should David: (a) check (b) bet \$1 (c) bet \$4?

(a) ☐	(b) ☐	(c) ☐	Points: ....

Action: David checked again, as did the machine.

River: A♦-K♦-J♦-4♥-7♣. David held Q♦-10♦.

Question 4: Should David: (a) check (b) bet \$1 (c) bet \$4?

(a) ☐	(b) ☐	(c) ☐	Points: ....
			Total: ....

Action: David bet $1 and the machine passed.

Now that is what I call a bad beat story. A royal flush on your very first hand, but you win no money and cannot even get a computer to play against you.

I thought that this was the worst possible beat. However, in 2002, I was showing my 12-year-old great nephew Ben the elements of poker. After the session, his six-year-old sister Lisa insisted on playing. Of course, I could only show her the various hands, not the concept of betting.

After a few hands I dealt myself a nine-high straight flush. Again, it wasn't for money and this time there was nobody else around to appreciate that I had hit a 65,000/1 shot!

SCORECHART

40 I trust that was your score.

30-39 David scored 33, but there was a special reason. David M and Danny made the same score.

15-29 Did you keep becoming impatient?

3-14 Oh, come on. You're kidding! Lisa would have done better than this.

ANSWERS AND ANALYSIS

Holding: Q♦-10♦

Answer 1: (a) 0 (b) 3 (c) 3 (d) 10.

This is a very strong hand in a two-handed game.

Flop: A♦-K♦-J♦.

Answer 2: (a) 10 (b) 0 (c) 0.

The machine was programmed to bluff about 5% of the time. Alternatively, it must be given a chance to try and catch up.

Turn: A♦-K♦-J♦-4♥.

Answer 3: (a) 10 (b) 1 (c) 1.

Nothing has changed.

River: A♦-K♦-J♦-4♥ 7♣.

Answer 4: (a) 4 (b) 10 (c) 3.

The machine is just going to check it right back. It is best to give it the maximum pot odds to make a call.

Hand 14

Vigour

INTRODUCTION

This was a £100 buy-in game at the Victoria with £1-£1 blinds. I have always believed that the common international practice of £1-£2 blinds is superior, but that is the custom that has grown up at the 'Vic'. It makes little difference in Omaha, since one can usually find an excuse for calling an extra £1 from the small blind in that game. In hold'em, however, it simply means that there should be a raise before the flop to cut out the two tourists. They may just be there because they have paid the forced blinds.

Three players had called for £1, including Mark. The late David Spanier held Q♣-J♣ in late position. The pot was £5 and it was £1 to him.

THE PLAY

Question 1: Should David: (a) pass (b) call (c) raise £1 (d) raise £6?

(a) ☐	(b) ☐	(c) ☐	(d) ☐	Points: ....

Action: David raised £6. Nobody else showed any interest and soon it was down to two-handed between David and Mark. David had successfully achieved his objective of sending the tourists packing. He also had position; second to speak.

Flop: 10♣-9♣-3♦. David held Q♣-J♣ and the pot stood at £18. Mark now bet the full £18, bringing the pot up to £36.

Question 2: Should David: (a) pass (b) call (c) raise £18 (d) raise £54?

(a) ☐	(b) ☐	(c) ☐	(d) ☐	Points: ....

Action: David called.

Turn: 10♣-9♣-3♦-6♥. David held Q♣-J♣. Mark now checked. The pot was £54.

Question 3: Should David: (a) check (b) bet £18 (c) bet £54?

(a) ☐	(b) ☐	(c) ☐	Points: ....

Action: David bet £54 and Mark raised £150. The pot stood at £312 and Mark had £300 left.

Question 4: Should David: (a) pass (b) call (c) raise £150 (d) raise £450?

(a) ☐	(b) ☐	(c) ☐	(d) ☐	Points: ....

Action: David called.

River: 10♣-9♣-3♦-6♥-A♠. David held Q♣-J♣. Mark checked. The pot was £462.

Question 5: Should David: (a) check (b) bet £150 (c) bet £450?

(a) ☐	(b) ☐	(c) ☐	Points: ....

Action: David checked and Mark showed the nuts, 8♥-7♥. Perhaps he played rather loosely initially, but he certainly made the most of his good fortune.

David wrote up this hand for his weekly poker column in *The Independent*, a national British newspaper. I have a confession to make: although I read it at the time, I did not take any notes. Thus I have somewhat embroidered the truth.

David was an excellent writer who authored three poker books: *Total Poker*, *The Little Book of Poker*, and *The Hand I Played*. The latter was published posthumously. He was also a delightful dinner companion. He asked me what I thought of his play in this hand. I shook my head sadly. He said, 'Yes, I know.'

Question 6: What should Mark have done, had David raised on the flop, making it £54 to go in a £108 pot: (a) pass (b) call (c) raise £54 (d) raise £162?

(a) ☐	(b) ☐	(c) ☐	(d) ☐	Points: ....
				Total: ....

SCORECHART

60 Proper, faultless aggressive play. This is what David M, Danny and I all achieved.

50-59 Highly satisfactory.

35-49 David S scored 43. He tried to recover from his error on the flop.

20-34 What have you done?

0-19 A calamity! Have a nice cup of tea.

ANSWERS AND ANALYSIS

Holding: Q♣-J♣.

Answer 1: (a) -1 (b) 10 (c) 2 (d) 8.

David has a pretty fair hand, but not a premium one. He was not a pushy player; it would make more sense for me to raise than for him to do so.

Flop: 10♣-9♣-3♦.

Answer 2: (a) -5 (b) 0 (c) 2 (d) 10.

This is a premium hand. David could make a straight flush, a flush, two straights or two overpairs, all of which figure to be winning.

Turn: 10♣-9♣-3♦-6♥.

Answer 3: (a) 10 (b) 0 (c) 5.

David still has a good hand. However, he is probably behind and is unlikely to secure a pass, not having shown strength on the flop. It is better to check and hope to improve. If he fails to do so, he can go quietly into the night.

Answer 4: (a) 0 (b) 10 (c) 0 (d) 1.

David still had 15 outs: nine clubs, three kings and three eights. In addition, any queen or jack might still win. Even if Mark held 8♣-7♣, David would still have the pot odds to call. There are also the imponderable implied odds. How much extra might he win were he to hit his hand?

River: 10♣-9♣-3♦-6♥-A♠.

Answer 5: (a) 10 (b) -2 (c) 2.

Mark showed strength on the turn, and he may be afraid that David has A-10. However, he is probably going to call anyway, so a sheepish check is required.

Answer 6: (a) 10 (b) 3 (c) 0 (d) 0.

I do not know Mark, but he is obviously a player much to be respected. He would have passed, since all he has is the ignorant end of the straight. That is, a jack does not necessarily give him the winning hand, so he only has three nut outs. The importance of nut outs is less in hold'em than in Omaha, but they still count for something. He could not expect that an eight or seven would give him the winning hand.

Had he made the mistake of calling and then checking the turn, then David could have checked right back. It would have been cheaper to play the hand this way.

You may like to know the percentage chance of winning against certain hands on the flop had you been in David's shoes:

Q♣-J♣ against A♠-10♦. Q♣-J♣ wins 69%.

Q♣-J♣ against 10♠-9♥. Q♣-J♣ wins 53%.

Q♣-J♣ against 10♦-10♥. Q♣-J♣ wins 42%.

Q♣-J♣ against A♣-K♣. Q♣-J♣ wins 40%.

Q♣-J♣ against K♣-8♣. Q♣-J♣ wins 36%.

Of course, there is no way *anyone* could know that K♣-8♣ was the best possible hand to have against David in this situation. A player might well pass this hand. The reason for this apparent paradox is that the K♣-8♣ dominates David's draw and also reduces his number of outs. Domination is a particularly important concept in hold'em.

The probabilities quoted are courtesy of Dr Mahmood Mahmood's program *Fastpoker*. His book *The Science of Poker* is a mine of useful information.

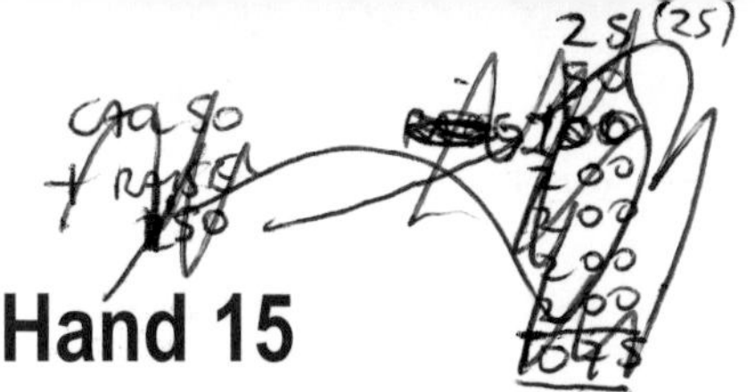

Hand 15

Don't be impatient

INTRODUCTION

This hand, which Bob Ciaffone wrote about briefly in our book, *Pot-Limit and No-Limit Poker*, was played some years ago in Las Vegas. It was a $1000 buy-in cash game, but everyone had much more than that on the table. The blinds were $25-$50 and I was first to speak with A♥-K♠.

THE PLAY

Question 1: Should I: (a) pass (b) call $50 (c) raise to $100 (d) raise to $200? (In this game, pre-flop raises were calculated as if the small blind had already made up the blind to $50.)

(a) ☐	(b) ☐	(c) ☐	(d) ☐	Points: ....

Action: I made it $200 to go. Anyone who has read my Omaha book will not be surprised by this; I am used to leading from the front. Anyway, this particular line-up of players would have been perfectly happy to limp in. They would only tangle with me by raising with what they believed to be the better hand.

Four players called and both blinds passed.

Flop: K♥-10♦-7♥. I held A♥-K♠ and there was $1075 in the pot.

Question 2: Should I: (a) check (b) bet $200 (c) bet $1075?

(a) ☐	(b) ☐	(c) ☐	Points: ....

Action: I bet $1000. Carl, an extremely experienced and strong player, now raised $3000 immediately after me. He now had $8500 left.

Hypothetical Action: What if a third player had now called?

Question 3: Should I: (a) pass (b) call (c) raise the pot?

(a) ☐	(b) ☐	(c) ☐	Points: ....

Returning to real life, where I was just facing Carl's raise:

Flop: K♥-10♦-7♥. I held A♥-K♠. There was $6075 in the pot and I was facing a bet of $3000.

Question 4: Should I: (a) pass (b) call (c) raise $8500 all-in?

(a) ☐ (b) ☐ (c) ☐ Points: ....

Hypothetical Hand: I hold A♠-K♠ and the flop is K♥-10♦-7♥.

Question 5: Should I: (a) pass (b) call (c) raise $8500 all-in?

(a) ☐ (b) ☐ (c) ☐ Points: ....

Now we return to the actual hand.

Turn: K♥-10♦-7♥-4♠. I held A♥-K♠. The pot stood at $9075 and Carl had $8500 left.

Question 6: Should I: (a) check (b) bet $3000 (c) bet $8500?

(a) ☐ (b) ☐ (c) ☐ Points: ....

Action: I set Carl in. He called and I turned my hand over. The last card was a blank and I won a chunky pot.

Later that day, Carl and I discussed this hand. He said that he had played it badly and should not have raised out of position. He did not volunteer what he actually held and I did not like to ask. Players often become very upset if one insists on seeing their hole cards when they have conceded the pot. Also it is poor percentage play, since they may have misread their hand and actually be winning!

Hypothetical Turn: K♥-10♦-7♥-4♥. I held A♥-K♠. The pot stands at $9075.

Question 7: Should I: (a) check (b) bet $5000 (c) bet $8500?

(a) ☐ (b) ☐ (c) ☐ Points: ....

Hypothetical Action: I check and Carl goes all-in for $8500.

Question 8: Should I: (a) pass (b) call?

(a) ☐ (b) ☐ Points: ....

Total: ....

SCORECHART

80 Find yourself a different game from mine.

70-79 I still want to avoid you. David, Danny and I all scored 78.

55-69 Well, this was an extremely difficult hand to play. My scoring was partly determined by the fact that I got it right.

40-54 There is certainly still room for improvement.

20-39 You must develop greater empathy with what your opponent is up to.

3-19 The hand is probably simply beyond your level of understanding.

ANSWERS AND ANALYSIS

Holding: A♥-K♠.

Answer 1: (a) 0 (b) 10 (c) 3 (d) 8.

This is a pretty good hand, ranking fifth in my opinion. Most of the time this is good enough to be the best hand before the flop, even though none of eight opponents have given any indication of the strength of their hand. However, I have poor position, so it is probably best simply to call.

Flop: K♥-10♦-7♥.

Answer 2: (a) 2 (b) 0 (c) 10.

My hand still reckons to be winning. If you checked with the intention of raising a bet, then you can award yourself five points. However, I do not think this is best play. Before you know it, you may be all-in with the inferior hand. It is better to bet out and, if raised, take stock. This is a dangerous board with which to give a free card.

Answer 3: (a) 10 (b) 2 (c) 0.

It is unlikely that two opponents can each have big draws, so one or both must have me beaten. It is true that I am being offered better odds with two opponents rather than one. However, the downside is that I am much less likely to win. After all, one opponent may have A-K with me.

Answer 4: (a) 4 (b) 10 (c) 0.

From the point of view of the other players, it was most unlikely that my first $1000 bet was a bluff. Thus my poorest holding had to be K-Q or perhaps A♥-Q♥. Similarly, it is impossible that Carl was bluffing, since there were three other players yet to act.

What can Carl reasonably have? I assume he would have passed K-7 or 10-7 before the flop and that he would often slowplay trips.

WARNING: Complex maths follows

Hand	**Relative Probability of holding this Hand**
Trips	7
K-10	6
A-A	3
A-K	6
K-Q	8
Q♥-J♥, Q♥-10♥, J♥-10♥, 10♥-9♥ or 9♥-8♥	5
Total number of hands	**35**

Obviously I did not figure this out at the table. How did I do so for the book?

There is only one combination for trip kings and three combinations for each of a set of tens or sevens. There are six ways that K-10 can be put together and so on down the list. It impossible to estimate how likely it is that Carl would have raised with just K-Q. You will note that I have dismissed K-J as a possibility altogether.

I am splitting the pot with six of the hands, which I shall treat as if they were three wins, and I am winning against K-Q or any of the flush draws in the bottom line of the table. Thus I am winning with 16/35 hands and it is clearly wrong to pass. It is true that I will be outdrawn by some of the drawing hands, but, to set against that, there is the extra money I can win.

Answer 5: (a) 0 (b) 10 (c) 0.

Since I don't have the A♥ in this example, the probability that Carl has A♥-X♥ is very high indeed.

But, returning to the actual hand, why not raise all-in? This would avoid making a mistake later in the pot. Well, be patient, that is explained on the turn.

Turn: K♥-10♦-7♥-4♠.

Answer 6: (a) 2 (b) 0 (c) 10.

If he is drawing then I am now big favourite. If he has K-Q, he is more likely to call than if I had raised all-in on the flop. If I am losing, well goodnight and sweet dreams. He is not about to pass.

Answer 7: (a) 10 (b) 3 (c) 8.

Here I can check, when he may think that I am slowplaying the nuts and check right back. He may also have made a flush and decide to give me a free card, in which case I am not drawing dead. By the way, if he has made a flush, the chance of my successfully bluffing the nut flush is slight. He would hardly have raised the flop in order to pass his hand once he has made it. Instead of checking, I can bet $5000 to give the impression that I am trying to keep him in, or I can bet all-in and, if called, rely on my flush outs.

By delaying the moment of truth until the turn, I leave myself more options.

Answer 8: (a) 10 (b) 0.

It is inconceivable to me that such a strong player would risk setting me in with less than A-K. Even if he does not have a flush, I only have nine wins out of 46. The odds are woefully inadequate.

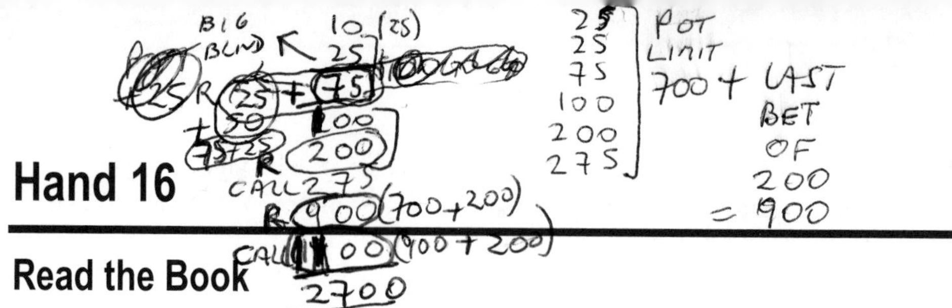

Hand 16

Read the Book

INTRODUCTION

Here is another hand that was played in Las Vegas. The blinds were $10-$25. I was in the big blind and Carl in the small. Everyone passed around to Fiery, who made it $100 to go on the button. Carl raised $200. Thus the pot stood at $425 and it was $275 to me if I wished to call.

I held Q♥-Q♦. Fiery had only just recently come to the table, but I did not give him that name accidentally.

THE PLAY

Question 1: Should I: (a) pass (b) call (c) raise $300 (d) raise $700?

(a) ☐	(b) ☐	(c) ☐	(d) ☐	Points: ....

Action: I called. Fiery raised a further $900 and Carl called. Thus the pot stood at $2700 and it was $900 to me. All three of us had ample funds to fight the good fight.

Question 2: Should I: (a) pass (b) call (c) raise $900 (d) raise $3600?

(a) ☐	(b) ☐	(c) ☐	(d) ☐	Points: ....

Action: I called.

Flop: 10♠-9♠-3♦. I held Q♥-Q♦. Carl checked and the pot stood at $3600.

Question 3: Should I: (a) check (b) bet $1000 (c) bet $3600?

(a) ☐	(b) ☐	(c) ☐	Points: ....

Action: I checked, Fiery bet $3600 and Carl passed. I had $12,000 left.

Question 4: Should I: (a) pass (b) call (c) raise $8400 all-in?

(a) ☐	(b) ☐	(c) ☐	Points: ....

Action: I passed and that was the end of it. The sheer weight of money had influenced my decision, and something else that we will come to presently.

Shortly afterwards Carl and I discussed this hand in whispers. Fiery was on the other side of the dealer and could not hear. I had written Carl a note, guessing at his hand and telling him mine.

Question 5: What hand did I think Carl held: (a) A-A (b) K-K (c) Q-Q (d) A-K (e) J-J (f) something else?

(a) ☐	(b) ☐	(c) ☐	(d) ☐	(e) ☐	(f) ☐	Points: ....
						Total: ....

SCORECHART

50 Very impressive.

40-49 Excellent. I scored 47, David 41 and Danny 40. It is easier to raise at the end, three years later and with no money at stake.

30-39 Another difficult hand. The correct play is only my opinion.

15-29 This is becoming a bit feeble.

0-14 You are not a first-class poker player – yet. Keep trying.

ANSWERS AND ANALYSIS

Holding: Q♥-Q♦.

Answer 1: (a) 2 (b) 10 (c) 0 (d) 5.

Normally I would be extremely cautious when facing a second raise from someone who plays as well as Carl. However, the act of raising someone as aggressive as Fiery is little more than a first raise. Neither of them had any reason to believe that I would be interested in the pot.

Answer 2: (a) 6 (b) 10 (c) 0 (d) 0.

Although the pot is now much bigger, nothing much has changed. Carl may be worried about my holding, or he may have pocket aces or kings and be slowplaying in order to trap me.

There is some merit to reraising in order to try to isolate myself against Fiery, but Q-Q is not an ideal holding for this play.

Flop: 10♠-9♠-3♦.

Answer 3: (a) 10 (b) 0 (c) 0.

Fiery is probably going to bet and I should not try to stop him. Once he has done so, if Carl calls, I can be satisfied that I am not winning, and pass.

Answer 4: (a) 7 (b) 0 (c) 10.

I still do not know where I am against Fiery. He could have a hand such as A♠-K♠, which would actually be favourite against my hand, although not by anything near 2/1. We have arrived at the combustion point – the time has come to either put up or shut up.

Answer 5: (a) -4 (b) 5 (c) 10 (d) 5 (e) 1 (f) 4.

That is correct. I thought that Carl held the statistically improbable case pair of queens and he confirmed to me I was correct. Of course, he may have been lying! This reading of his cards inhibited my play. It meant that there was no way I could improve. Also, the fact that neither he nor I held an ace or king made it more likely that they would be found in Fiery's hand.

However, my approach was totally illogical. I would not be calling in the vain hope that I could outdraw Fiery if necessary. My experience in Omaha had got the better of me. In that game, the possibility that some of your cards are matched is terribly important.

Once again, we see what a valuable weapon the button can be.

Fiery's aggressive ways continued unabated in that game. I have forgotten how the three of us fared overall.

Hand 17

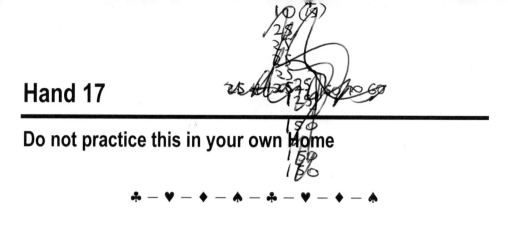

Do not practice this in your own Home

♣ – ♥ – ♦ – ♠ – ♣ – ♥ – ♦ – ♠

INTRODUCTION

This encounter took place in Las Vegas, where I have played most of my pot-limit hold'em of recent years. The game was $10-$25 blinds.

I was in seat 8 with A♥-J♥, and three people had already called in front of me. It was $25 to me and there was $110 in the pot.

THE PLAY

Question 1: Should I: (a) pass (b) call (c) raise $25 (d) raise $150?

(a) ☐	(b) ☐	(c) ☐	(d) ☐	Points: ....

Action: I raised the full $150 and only the small blind and two other people called. I had thus narrowed down the field and won the button.

Flop: 9♦-8♠-4♦. I held A♥-J♥ and the pot was $750. The first player checked and Liam, second in hand, bet the full $750. The third player folded. Liam was a sensible, aggressive, moderately experienced player. Both he and I had ample funds.

Hypothetical Action: What if the third player had called?

Question 2: Should I: (a) pass (b) call (c) raise $750 (d) raise $3000?

(a) ☐	(b) ☐	(c) ☐	(d) ☐	Points: ....

Returning to the actual hand:

Question 3: Given that Liam has bet the third player out, should I: (a) pass (b) call (c) raise $750 (d) raise $2250?

(a) ☐	(b) ☐	(c) ☐	(d) ☐	Points: ....

Action: I called $750 and the first player passed.

Turn: 9♦-8♠-4♦-3♣. I held A♥-J♥ and the pot was $2250. Liam bet $2000, bringing the pot up to $4250.

Question 4: Should I: (a) pass (b) call (c) raise $2000 (d) raise $6000?

(a) ☐	(b) ☐	(c) ☐	(d) ☐	Points: ....

Action: I called.

River: 9♦-8♠-4♦-3♣-3♥. I held A♥-J♥. The pot was $6250, into which Liam now bet a further $6000.

Question 5: Should I: (a) pass (b) call (c) raise $4000 all-in?

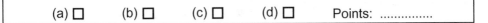

(a) ☐	(b) ☐	(c) ☐	Points: ....
			Total: ....

Action: I called. He said, 'You win,' and may have thrown his cards away. Anyway, I showed my hand and claimed the pot.

Would I have scored it the same way had he turned over a winner? The answer is probably yes. Changing the analysis to fit the result is one of the easiest traps for commentators to fall into. However, I doubt that I would have included it in my anthology of memorable hands.

One of the disadvantages of playing in this manner, is that it is then difficult to maintain a low profile. In my book, *Starting out in Poker*, I describe six types of player:

- ♦ Soft, loose
- ♦ Hard, loose
- ♦ Boss
- ♦ Soft, tight
- ♦ Hard, tight
- ♦ Anonymous

You do not want to be one of the first two, but you would like to create such an image. However, it is difficult to achieve a 'soft' image without actually giving away money. Playing a hand in this manner (or the way I played Hand 15) makes it impossible to remain anonymous. Good players are going to remember what went on.

It is interesting to note how most people would play a picture pair here. They would probably raise either on the flop or the turn and win less money.

SCORECHART

50 This is what I scored. Next time, both you and I may get egg all over our faces.

40-49 David's score. A highly satisfactory result.

25-39 Danny scored 27. You may have played in too timidly, or alternatively in an over-aggressive fashion.

10-24 You need to do more homework.

0-9 Much, much more homework.

♣ — ♥ — ♦ — ♠ — ♣ — ♥ — ♦ — ♠

ANSWERS AND ANALYSIS

Holding: A♥-J♥.

Answer 1: (a) -1 (b) 5 (c) 2 (d) 10.

This is quite a good playing hand, ranking seventh in my opinion. It figures to be best at this stage and, if back-raised, I can always pass. Furthermore, by raising I may drive out the button and thus claim it for myself.

Flop: 9♦-8♠-4♦.

Answer 2: (a) 10 (b) 0 (c) -2 (d) -5.

I have no pair and am trying to run over two players. That would be stupid.

Answer 3: (a) 6 (b) 10 (c) -2 (d) -1.

It is certainly circumspect to pass. Raising would be crazy, and we have yet to find out whether the original small blind is interested in the pot. Why did Liam bet? Traditionally he should check and let the original raiser go to work. Perhaps he has a drawing hand and is perfectly happy to contest the pot, but would like it still better if he were to win it there and then.

Turn: 9♦-8♠-4♦-3♣.

Answer 4: (a) 8 (b) 10 (c) -2 (d) -1.

There is no reason to change my mind. Liam may still be on a draw and now be trying to steal the pot. However, he seems extremely determined. Normally a pass would be in order, since there is no need to be rigid and automatically call all bets. Raising is much too dangerous. It may succeed against A-9, but why raise someone if you started out with the idea that they were bluffing?

River: 9♦-8♠-4♦-3♣-3♥.

Answer 5: (a) 4 (b) 10 (c) 1.

Of course it is not too late to pass, but I should really have decided to do that on the turn, not now. Is he really betting a hand like A-9? No, he would be happy just to check and show that down. If I then bet, he could make a decision whether to pass or call, hoping that I was bluffing. It would be sending a boy on a man's errand to raise all-in. Representing a very high pair might work, but he is only too liable to call because of the pot odds.

I may well have hesitated on the flop and/or the turn. Well, I had good reason to do so; my hand was not very strong. Such uncertainty has the advantage that it is more likely to engender a bluff. However, it has the disadvantage that it may cause an opponent to bet a weak, but winning hand.

Hand 18

Should you make your Excuses and leave?

INTRODUCTION

Fred asked me my opinion of the following hand, which he played in a tournament. Truth to tell, it was no-limit, but it is easy to adapt.

There were still several tables in action. The blinds were a notional £25-£50. Three people had called and Fred was on the button with A♠-A♣. It was £50 to him and the pot stood at £225.

THE PLAY

Question 1: Should he: (a) pass (b) call (c) raise £50 (d) raise £275? (In tournaments it is rare to assume that the small blind had been made up to £50 for the purposes of calculating a pre-flop raise.)

(a) ☐	(b) ☐	(c) ☐	(d) ☐	Points: ....

Action: Fred raised £200. The two blinds passed, as did one of the callers. Thus there were two opponents, Ann and Bert, in for the flop.

Flop: 10♦-9♠-3♦. Fred held A♠-A♣. The pot stood at £875.

Hypothetical Action: Both players check to Fred.

Question 2: Should Fred: (a) check (b) bet £200 (c) bet £875?

(a) ☐	(b) ☐	(c) ☐	Points: ....

Hypothetical Action: Fred bets £800, Ann raises £2400 and Bert comes over the top raising everybody £5000 all-in. The pot is £13,075 and it is £7400 to Fred.

Question 3: Should Fred: (a) pass (b) call?

(a) ☐	(b) ☐	Points: ....

Returning to the actual hand. To remind you, the flop was 10♦-9♠-3♦ and Fred held A♠-A♣.

Action: Ann bet £800 and the Bert raised £2400. The pot stood at £4875 and it was £3200 to Fred. Were he to call there would be £5000 action left.

Question 4: Should Fred: (a) pass (b) call (c) raise £5000 all-in?

(a) ☐	(b) ☐	(c) ☐	Points: ....

Action: Fred called, Ann raised all-in £5000 and Bert called.

The pot stood at £20,475. It was £5000 to Fred.

Question 5: Should Fred: (a) pass (b) call?

(a) ☐	(b) ☐	Points: ....

Action: Fred called. Both players turned out to have 10-9 and Fred did not improve, so he was out of the tournament.

Hypothetical Question 6: If both players gone mad and shown their two pair before Fred had made the final call, should he: (a) pass (b) call?

(a) ☐	(b) ☐	Points: ....
		Total: ....

SCORECHART

60 Like Fred, you would have lost the lot. David achieved this score.

55-59 Possibly superior play. I am not sure what I would have done in an actual event, so I would have scored either 57 or 60. Danny made 57.

40-54 Presumably you ignored the check-raise warning sign.

20-39 Play small stakes poker only.

0-19 What are you playing at?

ANSWERS AND ANALYSIS

Holding: A♠-A♣.

Answer 1: (a) -5 (b) 2 (c) 4 (d) 10.

It is possible to slowplay pocket aces, but there are already three volunteers in the pot, quite apart from the two tourists. Just because Fred raises the maximum does not mean that he must have the ultimate powerhouse.

Flop: 10♦-9♠-3♦.

Answer 2: (a) 0 (b) 1 (c) 10.

Fred must reckon that he is winning, and it is too dangerous to give a free card with two diamonds and also connectors on the flop.

Answer 3: (a) 10 (b) 1.

Both opponents have decided that they liked their hand enough to check-raise. Whenever someone check-raises they are suggesting that they hold a powerhouse. The second player must have a made hand. If he were drawing, surely he would want Fred in? Moreover, he is risking his place in the tournament. If he does have the mythic Q♦-J♦, then he is favourite against Fred and there is still Ann to contend with. It is correct for Fred to pass.

Answer 4: (a) 7 (b) 10 (c) 2.

This is a really difficult decision even if one knows the punters. Ann may well be betting on the come, whereas Bert may be raising with perhaps J-10 in order to isolate himself with the bettor. On the other hand, they may both be caked up.

There seems to be no merit in reraising. That will not affect Ann's decision whether to pass or call on the flop. The combustion point has not yet arrived yet, from Fred's viewpoint. He can await developments.

Answer 5: (a) 0 (b) 10.

Fred has been whip-lashed, but it is too late to turn back now.

Answer 6: (a) 0 (b) 10.

He is better than 3/1 against and gets 4/1 for his chips. You will not win tournaments by waiting until you have a bigger overlay than that.

By the way, showing your cards in that way would not be allowed in England. At one time it would even have lost you the pot at the World Series of Poker, although I do not know if this is the current rule.

Once all the action is complete in a tournament, the hands are put on their backs and the remaining cards are dealt. Thus everybody knows what is going on. I would like to see this in money poker as well, but that is not the way it is done.

Hand 19

Not my Cup of Tea

INTRODUCTION

I thought I had retired from tournament play, since I have never done particularly well in such events and I do not relish the potentially long sessions and cigarette smoke. However, as far as I can recall, I have never actually played in a pot-limit hold'em tournament. So when a small one was held at the Grosvenor Victoria in April 2003, I thought I owed it to my readers to play. It was unlikely that the event would last for more than six hours.

The entry fee was £50 with a £5 administration charge, for which we received 2000 chips. As you will have noticed, I have referred to the chips in a tournament as if they were £s or $s, rather than just numbers. This is simply for the convenience of anyone who just leafs through the book and would otherwise become confused.

Re-buys were allowed for the first hour. The re-buys cost only £50 and thus were £5 cheaper than the original buy-in. The opportunity to re-buy changes the strategy; you are not playing for your life during this period. However, the aim must be to amass chips as cheaply as possible. Of course, I had a somewhat different objective: to play to last so that I could write notes for this book. It was also difficult for me to take such a low stakes event seriously, but that is my fault.

This hand occurred in the re-buy period. The blinds were £25-£50. Fred had made it £175 to go and The Inventor had called. The small blind then passed, so there was £425 in the middle and it was £125 to John, holding Q♥-J♦ in the big blind.

THE PLAY

Question 1: Should John: (a) pass (b) call (c) raise £125 (c) raise £550?

(a) ☐	(b) ☐	(c) ☐	Points: ....

Action: John called.

Flop: Q♣-10♣-8♣. John held Q♥-J♦. The pot was £550 and all three players had about £2000 left in chips.

Question 2: Should John: (a) check (b) bet £150 (c) bet £550?

(a) ☐	(b) ☐	(c) ☐	Points: ....

Action: John bet £500. Fred now raised £1500 all-in and The Inventor called all-in. The pot stood at £5050 and it was £1500 to John.

Question 3: Should John: (a) pass (b) call?

(a) ☐	(b) ☐	Points: ....

Hypothetical Action: John bets £150 on the flop and Fred raises £850. Thus it is £1000 to The Inventor and he calls. The pot is now £2700. It is £850 to John, who still has £1850 in chips.

Question 4: Should John: (a) pass (b) call (c) raise all-in for £1000 more?

(a) ☐	(b) ☐	(c) ☐	Points: ....

Hypothetical Action: John decides to call.

Hypothetical Turn 1: Q♣-10♣-8♣-7♣. John holds Q♥-J♦.

Question 5: Should John: (a) check (b) bet £500 (c) bet £1000 all-in?

(a) ☐	(b) ☐	(c) ☐	Points: ....

Hypothetical Turn 2: Q♣-10♣-8♣-2♦. John holds Q♥-J♦.

Question 6: Should John: (a) check (b) bet £500 (c) bet £1000 all-in?

(a) ☐	(b) ☐	(c) ☐	Points: ....

Let us return to the actual hand.

Action: On the day, John called all-in, having himself bet out £500 on the flop. John held Q♥-J♦, Fred A♣-3♠ and The Inventor 9♣-8♦. As the cards were put on their backs, John said, 'Well, I'm quite satisfied with my play so far.'

Flop, Turn and River: Q♣-10♣-8♣-8♥-4♥. Thus The Inventor won a £6700 pot. He had already bought in once, but did not have to do so again. He presumably became temporary chip leader for the whole room. However, he didn't seem to notice how big an outdraw this was.

Question 7: John did not buy in again. Was this correct general strategy: (a) yes (b) maybe (c) no?

(a) ☐	(b) ☐	(c) ☐	Points: ....
			Total: ....

SCORECHART

70 Well done. David made this score. Did you feel a little like I did? That you would never have called the first bet and thus could not have got into a mess. Naturally I always tend to make a 100% score in the hands that I did not play!

60-69 Highly satisfactory.

45-59 Danny scored 53. That is how one gets knocked out of tournaments.

30-44 Play in smaller tournaments.

15-29 An awful result.

3-14 If you don't mind losing, then it is okay to enter a competition.

ANSWERS AND ANALYSIS

Holding: Q♥-J♦.

Answer 1: (a) 10 (b) 1 (c) 0 (d) 0.

This is a reasonable hand if you are trying to accumulate chips, but John is out of position. If there were no re-buys, he should definitely pass. As it is, calling with this type of hand defies the law of conservation of chips.

Flop: Q♣-10♣-8♣.

Answer 2: (a) 10 (b) 6 (c) 1.

This is a fair hand, but the flop is very dangerous. Even if John is winning, it is easy for him to be outdrawn. A small bet, to see how much interest there is from the other two, is quite a good idea.

Answer 3: (a) 10 (b) 5.

As so often in tournaments, it has all rapidly got out of hand. It is probably best to pass, since John may well be losing in one spot with the other player on a good draw. Of course, it is perfectly possible there is already a flush out there.

Answer 4: (a) 10 (b) 6 (c) 0.

It is a marginal pass, but John can call. This is certainly much better than raising.

Answer 5: (a) 10 (b) 0 (c) -5.

It is almost certain that at least one player has made a flush. John can check and pass any bet.

Answer 6: (a) 2 (b) 0 (c) 10.

Nothing has changed. If John was winning before, he is still winning. On the other hand, if he is up against drawing hands, then he has succeeded in shading the odds in a manner favourable to him.

Answer 7: (a) 0 (b) 3 (c) 10.

You should only enter a tournament if you think you have a reasonable edge (unless you are purely a recreational player or have a unique reason for playing, like I did). Since it cost £55 on the first occasion and it is only £50 now, there is no reason to quit. It was very early in the competition, so the problem of being a pauper in the game did not apply. I find it difficult to play when on short rations, whereas others thrive in this situation.

Presumably John had decided upon his re-buy strategy before the event. Thus I believe that he should not even have played his marginal hand before the flop. He disobeyed the law of conservation of chips at practically every stage. His Q-J was inadequate to speculate, and once he saw the flop, he faced difficult problems. This so often arises when you call on limited values in the first place. Again he should have passed here.

Hand 20

To play conservatively or vigorously? That is the Question!

For the first hour of the tournament that began in the previous hand, I hit nothing. My best hand was something like A-9. If this seems improbable, you should note that I junked small pairs as not worth considering. I had just lost my second buy-in of £50 when time was called for the end of the re-buy period. I could either stop now, buy £50 chips or buy £100 chips (one re-buy plus an add-on). Most of the players at my table did not have large stacks.

THE PLAY

Question 1: Should *I*: (a) quit (b) spend £50 (c) spend £100?

(a) ☐	(b) ☐	(c) ☐	Points: ....

Question 2: Should *you*: (a) quit (b) spend £50 (c) spend £100?

(a) ☐	(b) ☐	(c) ☐	Points: ....

Action: I purchased 4000 chips for £100. After that I no longer had to play poker for about two hours. However, soon afterwards I picked up pocket kings and outdrew pocket aces and from then on I could do nothing wrong. I always started with the best hand and it always stood up. No-one had that many chips and little finesse was required.

As players came and went, my stack became more and more menacing. Thus players would pass moderate hands rather than go heads-up with me. Eventually there were only two tables left and players began deliberately to play slowly in order to try to ensure that they were not the knocked out before the prizes. Naturally I had no interest in that problem.

Eventually we were down to one table, and I had virtually half the chips in play. For a long time I had no hand worth considering, although I occasionally won a small pot by default.

Action: The blinds were £1000-£2000. Everyone had passed to me on the button. I held 8♠-7♦. The pot was £3000 and it was £2000 to me.

Question 3: Should I: (a) pass (b) call (c) raise £2000 (d) raise £5000?

(a) ☐	(b) ☐	(c) ☐	(d) ☐	Points: ....

Action: I raised £5000 and the Alan called in the small blind. The big blind passed.

Flop: 9♣-6♥-2♥. I held 8♠-7♦. Alan went all-in for £9000, so the pot stood at £25,000.

Question 4: Should I: (a) pass (b) call?

(a) ☐	(b) ☐	Points: ....

Action: I called. He turned over A♠-K♦, which stood up.

Alan played the hand cleverly. He tempted the big blind in by not reraising all-in. Also I might well have passed his reraise before the flop if I had total junk. He was taking a considerable risk, but that may have been necessary in order to build a stack.

Question 5: What percentage of the time do you think I win the pot with these two hands after the flop: (a) 30% (b) 40% (c) 50% (d) 60%?

(a) ☐	(b) ☐	(c) ☐	(d) ☐	Points: ....
				Total: ....

SCORECHART

50 Better than I managed.

40-49 Both David and I scored 43. Danny scored 40.

25-39 Probably you were a bit confused.

15-24 This paints a discouraging picture.

4-14 Perhaps the theoretical discussion turned you off.

ANSWERS AND ANALYSIS

Holding: 8♠-7♦

Answer 1: (a) 0 (b) 2 (c) 10.

I had entered the event primarily as an investigative journalist.

Answer 2: (a) 2 (b) 10 (c) 10.

How should I know? However, you should not quit on the assumption that the cards are not going your way and you are therefore out of form. This is nonsense; the cards have no memory of what has gone before. Admittedly, if you do believe in form, then it may become a self-fulfilling prophecy and you should definitely not pull up more money. I play better with more money in front of me and thus bought two stacks. You will have to judge your own psychology.

Answer 3: (a) 10 (b) 2 (c) 5 (d) 8.

This is a moderate hand in the circumstances. Both players are likely to pass if I made a full raise. Calling or making a small raise would be rather odd. Neither player had enough money for me to be making a subtle play with a powerhouse.

Flop: 9♣-6♥-2♥.

Answer 4: (a) 0 (b) 10.

I have no idea what hand my opponent has, but my straight draw gives me good chances. The worst nightmare would be that he held 8♥-7♥, but you would never sleep at night if you always worried about that possibility.

Answer 5: (a) 0 (b) 5 (c) 10 (d) 3.

I simulated the hand on Dr Mahmood Mahmood's program. I was caught out here as I thought it would be about 40%, but in fact it is very close to even money. In any case, I would have played at 30%, though not getting my pot odds. I was entranced by the idea of knocking a player out and edging closer to first place.

Hand 21

I often regret not playing badly!

INTRODUCTION

We are still in the same tournament. The blinds remained at £1000-£2000 and I was still chip leader by a long way. Bill opened the betting, semi-limping in with £4000 and everyone passed to me. The pot stood at £7000, and both Colm and Kate were still to act. I held K♠-J♥.

THE PLAY

Question 1: Should I: (a) pass (b) call (c) raise £4000 (d) raise £11,000?

(a) ☐	(b) ☐	(c) ☐	(d) ☐	Points: ....

Action: I raised £11,000, making it £15,000 to go. Colm passed, but Kate called £15,000 and raised £37,000, leaving herself with only £6000 more. Both blinds passed. Bill called for £15,000 all-in. The pot stood at £89,000, of which Bill could win £52,000, and it was £37,000 to me.

Question 2: Should I: (a) pass (b) call (c) raise Kate £6000 all-in?

(a) ☐	(b) ☐	(c) ☐	Points: ....

Action: I passed. Kate held A♥-Q♠ and Bill A♠-8♦. I held K♠-J♥.

Flop, Turn and River: A♦-7♠-J♦-Q♣-10♠.

Thus I would have hit the nuts and eliminated two players in one fell swoop. Actually, with the hands my opponents held, I was only 3/2 against winning. But, if Kate had held the dominating A-K, I would have been a 3/1 dog.

Bill faced two players who had raised. There was £37,000 that he could possibly win, but it would cost him £15,000 to call. If I called, he could win a further £4000, but he would have to face down two opponents. Clearly he would prefer me to pass.

Question 3: Should Bill: (a) pass (b) call?

(a) ☐	(b) ☐	Points: ....
		Total: ....

SCORECHART

30 My sentiments exactly.

20-29 Perhaps you called at the end, or did not raise Bill. Either way, you would have done better than me financially. David scored 25.

10-19 Rather scruffy. Danny only scored 11.

3-9 How could you?

ANSWERS AND ANALYSIS

Holding: K♠-J♥.

Answer 1: (a) 0 (b) 5 (c) 0 (d) 10.

I do not know Bill well, but my hand figures to be beating him. K-J ranks fairly well down in the hold'em hand rankings, but I have such favourable chip position that few are going to want to enter into an argument with me.

Answer 2: (a) 10 (c) 0 (c) 1.

This is typical of tournament poker, whether it is pot-limit or no-limit. Much of the play has gone out of the game before we even see a flop. Clearly I am beaten in two spots.

What is amazing is that I thought so long over this obvious decision. Clearly I was entranced by the thought of setting two of the remaining players all-in, but this is ridiculous. I would be mortally wounded if I lost to Kate, and 5/2 odds are woefully inadequate in this situation. It may appear a bit better than that, but the last £6000 is sure to go in.

Answer 3: (a) 10 (b) 3.

Bill is only getting a little better than 5/2 for his money and may well be behind in two spots (in real life, of course, it proved to be only one). After I passed, he was a little more than 3/1 against, as the cards lay. Had I called, he would have been worse than a 4/1 dog. Moreover, he is risking elimination from the event. A £15,000 stack was enough to continue playing. His call smacked a little of unnecessary desperation.

From my point of view, it was a pity that Bill did not make it £7000 to go from the off. Then I would have just called and saved myself £8000 (assuming Kate raised behind me and I then folded).

Hand 22

The Extended Gap Concept

INTRODUCTION

The tournament continued and now we were down to just three players, Colm to my left and Kate to his left. I have known both players for many years, but I seldom play against them nowadays. I was still chip leader and Colm was looking distinctly thin on top.

The blinds were £2000-£4000 and I held A♠-Q♥.

THE PLAY

Hypothetical Question 1: Had I been in the small blind with Kate having passed, should I: (a) pass (b) call (c) raise £4000 (d) raise £8000?

(a) ☐	(b) ☐	(c) ☐	(d) ☐	Points: ....

Hypothetical Question 2: Had I been in the big blind, with Colm having raised the pot £10,000 and Kate having passed, then there would have been £20,000 in the pot and it would have been £10,000 to me. In this situation, should I: (a) pass (b) call (c) raise £10,000 (d) raise £15,000 all-in?

(a) ☐	(b) ☐	(c) ☐	(d) ☐	Points: ....

Let us now return to the actual hand.

Action: I was in the big blind. Colm raised £10,000 and Kate reraised £28,000 all-in. The pot stood at £60,000 and it was £38,000 to me. If I called, I would have had £20,000 left in chips. Colm had another £25,000 awaiting his final decision.

Question 3: Should I: (a) pass (b) call?

(a) ☐	(b) ☐	Points: ....
		Total: ....

Action: I passed, as did Colm, despite his low chips and the fact that he could win £60,000 for £25,000. After this hand I still had £58,000 in chips, Kate £60,000 and Colm £25,000.

Later that evening we discussed this hand. Kate wasn't certain, but thought she had been holding A♦-Q♦. Knowing that, and with the hindsight that Colm was going to pass, I should call. The likelihood of my losing to a flush is not that high.

SCORECHART

30 This is exactly the way I played at the table. I was very surprised and disappointed when Kate reraised. David made the same score.

20-29 Fair enough.

10-19 Did you play too passively or too defensively? Danny only scored 14.

0-9 Reread the chapter, cutting out the high-falutin theoretical stuff.

ANSWERS AND ANALYSIS

Holding: A♠-Q♥.

Answer 1: (a) -2 (b) 2 (c) 2 (d) 10.

My hand is about as good as it gets two-handed. Colm has position on me and it is best not to get tricky against such an experienced player. A full raise is called for.

WARNING: Complex maths follows

In this position, in any variation of poker, I should be raising with about the best 50% of the possible hands, whatever that 50% may be. This 50% includes the fraction I should be bluffing. Since Colm may reraise, I should only raise about 35%, if I had no bluff in my soul. Since I was in a very advantageous chip position, I could push out the boat and raise with 60% of my hands.

Answer 2: (a) 0 (b) 2 (c) 0 (d) 10.

My hand is good enough to take Colm on and he can only wound me, not really hurt me. I hope you would have raised.

We have now explored the 'gap concept' without ever having heard of the term, or even been aware that we were using it to solve this question. The gap concept is an idea that David Sklansky highlights in his excellent book, *Tournament Poker for Advanced Players*. In my opinion the concept is simply a general poker one and not one that is necessarily related just to tournaments or even just to hold'em.

Basically I should raise with 50% of all possible hands, *but* Colm has bet. Thus, I should assume that he himself holds a good hand. Taking into account the fact that there are two opponents in the pot who haven't made a move, his hand should be in the top 25% statistically. Then he is beating Kate and I individually 75% of the time and the two of us 50% overall.

Since the pot is £20,000 and it is £10,000 to me, I am getting 2/1 for a call. Thus I should be calling with a hand in the top (2 x 25)/3 = 16.67%. The difference between 50% and 16.67% is what David refers to, in a different manner, as the gap concept.

Thus I would have raised with any hand in the top 25%, perhaps a holding such as 9♣-8♦, but should now only call with a hand that is somewhat better than that, such as a small pair or 10♠-9♠.

Since I am prepared to call with any hand in the top 16.67%, I should be prepared to raise with any hand in the top half of that fraction, in other words, 8.33%, which might be a holding such as A♠-J♦ or 9♠-9♦. Since I held A♠-Q♥, it is totally clear that our gut feeling to set Colm in, is totally correct.

I found it surprising that David Sklansky wrote that most players have not grasped this basic principle of the gap concept. In my earlier works I have said something similar but simpler, 'You can bet with anything, but must have a reasonable hand to call.'

There is a problem in hold'em. What is the order of value of the hands? Going all-in, we know 2♠-2♣ is a little better than A♠-Q♥. However, the latter is a much superior *playing* hand. This difficulty does not exist in draw poker and that is why the concept appears as early as page 16 in my book, *Starting out in Poker*.

In Omaha the whole idea of the gap concept simply does not exist before the flop. Who can say whether Q♥-J♠-J♦-6♠ is better than 8♥-7♦-6♦-4♣? Of course, you could run out a computer simulation of the match-up, but that will only tell us about the all-in situation.

Answer 3: (a) 10 (b) 2.

We again apply the gap concept. Colm would raise with the top 25% of hands. Thus Kate should call with the top 15% of all hands, and reraise with the top 8% of hands, if I were not in the pot. Since I have taken no action whatsoever so far, I may have a powerhouse, so we can perhaps assume that she might take this into account and only raise with the top 6%. Remember that I am not getting 2/1 for my money here, but £60,000/£38,000, or slightly better than 3/2. In this instance I should pass all but the upper 40% of the top 6% of hands.

That is the top (6 x 0.4)% poker hands, which is 2.4%. This is almost precisely at the A♠-K♥ level, which is significantly better than my holding of A♠-Q♥. My gut feeling has led me in the right direction.

We do not have time to make such calculations at the tables. It is perfectly adequate to conclude Kate must have such a good hand that calling with A♠-Q♥ will be a losing play.

What started out as a hand that I was perfectly prepared to raise with provided it was in the top 50%, has become one that I am now only prepared to call with if it is in the top 2.4%.

Thus we see an example of the totally new term that I invented last night: the 'extended gap concept'. I would have preferred to call it the 'ratchet principle', but David got there first!

But, you might well argue, I thought we were playing poker? All you have been doing is arithmetic. Quite right too!

Colm is a tight player and he is short of chips, so I reckon that in fact he would probably only raise in the first place with the top 20% of hands. Kate knows this and would probably only raise with the top 5%. Thus I should call with the top 2%. I need a hand at least as good as A♠-K♠ to call.

This shows why, if the money is there, I should usually only put in the third raise with a pair of aces. But there is another consideration too. This was a tournament, so if I had called, Colm would probably pass all but a pair of aces. He would hope that I will pick off Kate and he would thus move up into second place without any further action on his part.

A final wrinkle (at last!). If I fold and Colm calls, than Kate may well win the hand and knock him out. Then I will move into a guaranteed second place without any danger, while remaining in fair shape to win. There was no contest. I should not even have thought about it and should have passed immediately.

Hand 23

Captured

INTRODUCTION

Our story continues. The blinds were still £2000-£4000 and the poker host was unused to such a long saga at the end. He began muttering about the tournament having to finish by the time the casino closed at 4am. Was there some objection to our continuing to play real poker instead of hurtling in our chips?

I held 10♠-9♦ in the small blind with Kate having passed on the button. The pot stood at £6000 and it was £2000 to call.

THE PLAY

Question 1: Should I: (a) pass (b) call (c) raise £4000 (d) raise £8000?

(a) ☐	(b) ☐	(c) ☐	(d) ☐	Points: ....

Action: I raised £8000. At this point Colm had £45,000 in chips and he decided to call.

Hypothetical Action: What if Colm had raised £24,000?

Question 2: Should I: (a) pass (b) call (c) raise him all-in?

(a) ☐	(b) ☐	(c) ☐	Points: ....

Hypothetical Flop: J♥-6♠-2♦. I held 10♠-9♦ with £24,000 in the pot after Colm's pre-flop call.

Question 3: Should I: (a) check (b) bet £10,000 (c) bet £24,000?

(a) ☐	(b) ☐	(c) ☐	Points: ....

Let us return to the actual hand.

Flop: 9♥-8♠-3♥. I held 10♠-9♦ and first to speak. The pot stood at £24,000, Colm had £37,000 left in chips and I had about £50,000.

Question 4: Should I: (a) check (b) bet £10,000 (c) bet £24,000?

(a) ☐	(b) ☐	(c) ☐	Points: ....

Action: I bet £24,000 and Colm raised £13,000 all-in. The pot stood at £85,000.

Question 5: Should I: (a) pass (b) call?

(a) ☐	(b) ☐	Points: ....
		Total: ....

The cards were on their backs and Colm held A♠-A♦. There was no improvement on the turn or the river and thus Colm had built his stack up nicely.

Note how cannily Colm played to double up. He slowplayed his pocket aces, which was the only way that he could get paid off.

While preparing the proofs of this book, I thought of another new concept: the reward/risk ratio. (Hold'em lends itself to theoretical considerations better than most forms of poker.)

Colm took a big risk in not re-raising me pre-flop, since I might have had a hand good enough to call a raise before the flop, but poor enough to pass on the flop. Alternatively, I might have outdrawn him. His reward was to double through.

The reward was £37,000. The risk of being outdrawn in this particular hand was 21%. I can hit a nine or ten on the turn or river. He could lose £61,000. 61,000 x 0.21 = £12,810. Thus the reward/risk ratio = 37,000/12,810 = 3/1 approximately.

We can regard this as being similar to implied odds, but it is concerned with slowplaying a hand. Whether 3/1 is sufficiently high or low to take such a risk is a moot point.

In any case I was now seriously wounded in the tournament. The remaining hands were uninteresting; I once again ran into aces and finished third. Eventually, Colm and Kate each held more or less the same number of chips, and they agreed to split the first and second prizes. For my part, I made a small profit on the evening and, of course, lived to tell the tale.

SCORECHART

50 Just like David and I – and we all came unstuck!

40-49 Pretty good.

25-39 Not good enough. Danny scored 30.

10-24 Come and play in our game.

0-9 Don't play poker for real money.

ANSWERS AND ANALYSIS

Holding: 10♠-9♦.

Answer 1: (a) 0 (b) 1 (c) 3 (d) 10.

Two-handed this is well within the win segment. It is in the top 20-25% of all hands.

Answer 2: (a) 10 (b) 0 (c) 2.

I had already made up my mind that if Colm made a pot raise, I would pass. The hand was just not good enough to go to war with.

Answer 3: (a) 10 (b) 0 (c) 3.

I had made up my mind that Colm must be beating my holding to have called me before the flop, and I did not want to bluff this particular pot.

Flop: 9♥-8♠-3♥.

Answer 4: (a) 0 (b) 2 (c) 10.

It is highly likely I am winning, but I certainly do not have a hand that is good enough to check. He will almost certainly check straight back and any high card may spell ruination for me. Also he may be playing for a flush or straight.

Answer 5: (a) -5 (b) 10.

Although I rather gloomily concluded that I must be losing, my pot odds are way too high to consider passing here.

Hand 24

A Familiar Conundrum

INTRODUCTION

The blinds were £1000-£2000 in the later stages of a small tournament. Ike had called all-in for £1600 and everyone else had passed. There was therefore a main pot of £4200 and a side pot of £400. David Moskovic held Q♠-10♦ in the small blind, with £6400 chips left. DW, with half the chips in the whole event, was in the big blind.

THE PLAY

Question 1: Should David: (a) pass (b) call £1000 (c) raise £2000 (d) raise £5400 all-in?

(a) ☐	(b) ☐	(c) ☐	(d) ☐	Points: ....

Action: David called.

Hypothetical Action: DW raises £5000 to put David all-in. The main pot is £4800 and side pot £5800.

Question 2: Should David: (a) pass (b) call?

(a) ☐	(b) ☐	Points: ....

Action: We now return to the actual hand, where DW checked.

Flop: 10♣-8♠-5♣. David held Q♠-10♦ with £5000 left in chips. The main pot held £4800 and the side pot £800.

Question 3: Should David: (a) check (b) bet £2000 (c) bet £5000 all-in?

(a) ☐	(b) ☐	(c) ☐	Points: ....

Hypothetical Action: David checks, as does DW.

Hypothetical Turn: 10♣-8♠-5♣-7♠. David holds Q♠-10♦.

Question 4: Should David: (a) check (b) bet £2000 (c) bet £5000 all-in?

(a) ☐	(b) ☐	(c) ☐	Points: ....

Hypothetical Action: Let us assume that David again checks.

Hypothetical River: 10♣-8♠-5♣-7♠-J♦. David holds Q♠-10♦.

Question 5: Should David: (a) check (b) bet £2000 (c) bet £5000 all-in?

(a) ☐	(b) ☐	(c) ☐	Points: ....

Hypothetical Action: David checks and DW sets him in for £5000.

Question 6: Should David: (a) pass (b) call?

(a) ☐	(b) ☐	Points: ....
		Total: ....

Returning to the actual hand.

Action: I am glad to be able to tell you that David went all-in on the flop. DW said, 'You look like you've seen a ghost, so you must have a hand. I pass.' David collected the £800 side pot and now had £5800 in chips. (DW in fact held 9♠-5♦.) The remaining two players now revealed their hands in preparation for the final two cards.

Turn and River: 10♣-8♠-5♣-7♠-J♦. David held Q♠-10♦ and Ike K♦-K♣.

Thus Ike was back in business with £4800. DW would actually have won the whole pot with his rather ridiculous holding, by making a straight on the river. Ike went on to do well in the tournament; indeed he finished higher than David.

After the showdown DW scolded David for betting him out of the hand. But he did not need to pass, after all, he did flop a pair of fives. Assuming that David was beating him with a higher pair, he probably still had five outs twice over to win, which is roughly a 4/1 shot. The odds are unattractive, but the chance of knocking two players out in one hand is enticing. The strategy of checking it out in order to knock out the all-in player is vastly overrated.

SCORECHART

60 David achieved this, and it was my score as well.

50-59 You probably let DW in. Well, it is only my view that you are wrong.

35-49 A rather messy approach to the late stages of a tournament.

20-34 Mediocre.

10-19 Very poor

0-9 Simply dreadful.

ANSWERS AND ANALYSIS

Holding: Q♠-10♦.

Answer 1: (a) 0 (b) 10 (c) -1 (d) -5.

Applying the gap concept, this hand is nowhere near good enough to raise with if Ike were to have any chips left. However, he is all-in. Nothing is known of DW's hand, but on the balance of statistical probabilities, David is likely to be stronger than DW.

Why give DW a free shot at the pot? In order to try and bust Ike. It was only £1000 for David to call in order to win a potential £4600, so his odds are much too good to consider passing. David can reasonably rely on DW not to raise, unless he has a strong holding. He is likely to tacitly agree to co-operate with David to try and bust Ike.

David would have had to have a very weak hand indeed to pass. Calling £1000, of which Ike can only get £600, is hardly feeding the bears.

Answer 2: (a) 10 (b) -5.

DW should not be bluffing in this situation, as the side pot is quite small. Both gap theory and common sense indicate that Q-10 is totally inadequate to take on the chip leader in this situation.

Flop: 10♣-8♠-5♣.

Answer 3: (a) 5 (b) 5 (c) 10.

David has hit top pair, good kicker, a very strong hand against only two opponents. He has to reckon that he is winning, probably against both opponents and very likely indeed against DW. It is a widely held opinion that you should check the pot out in this situation, effectively conspiring with the big stack to bust the all-in player. However, this concept is fallacious. There is a side pot of £800 to win, and why should David allow DW the chance to outdraw him? A timid bet would not hack it. DW could well have two clubs and try to outdraw David.

Answer 4: (a) 6 (b) 0 (c) 10.

It is even more likely that David is winning here. It is most unlikely that DW has made a straight and he may have a stupid hand like 6♣-2♣, in which case a bet may even elicit a call.

Answer 5: (a) 10 (b) 0 (c) -3.

It is too late to bet now. DW may have hit the front accidentally.

Answer 6: (a) 10 (b) -5.

DW clearly thinks that he is winning. The river card has most likely helped his hand. No more Mr Nice Guy.

Hand 25

Don't rock the Boat

INTRODUCTION

Back to cash games now. Sometimes the techniques used in a ring game are identical to those required for a tournament. Whenever the money is deep enough in a tournament, or it is still in the re-buy stage, then there may be no substantial difference in the strategy. This is an example of one such hand.

The blinds were £10-£20. Three players had limped in before Art, who was on the button with K♥-Q♥. The pot stood at £90 and it was £20 to Art.

THE PLAY

Question 1: Should Art: (a) pass (b) call (c) raise £20 (d) raise £110?

(a) ☐	(b) ☐	(c) ☐	(d) ☐	Points: ....

Action: Art raised £100. The small blind called, as did the three original limpers. Nobody's body language suggested that they were raring to go and really wanted to reraise.

Flop: Q♦-8♠-3♥. Art held K♥-Q♥. The pot stood at £620 and all four players checked to him.

Question 2: Should Art: (a) check (b) bet £200 (c) bet £600?

(a) ☐	(b) ☐	(c) ☐	Points: ....

Hypothetical Action: Art bets £600, Joe raises £1800, Fred calls and the other players pass. The pot stands at £6020 and it is £1800 to Art to call.

Question 3: Should Art: (a) pass (b) call (c) raise £1800 (d) raise £7200?

(a) ☐	(b) ☐	(c) ☐	(d) ☐	Points: ....

Let us go back to the actual hand.

Action: Art bet £600. Both Joe and Fred now called, and the other two players folded.

Turn: Q♦-8♠-3♥-5♥. Art held K♥-Q♥. The pot stood at £2420. Both Joe and Fred checked.

Question 4: Should Art: (a) check (b) bet £600 (c) bet £2400?

(a) ☐	(b) ☐	(c) ☐	Points: ....

Action: Art checked.

River: Q♦-8♠-3♥-5♥-10♥. Art held K♥-Q♥ with £2420 in the pot. Both players again checked to Art.

Question 5: Should Art: (a) check (b) bet £600 (c) bet £1500 (d) bet £2400?

(a) ☐	(b) ☐	(c) ☐	(d) ☐	Points: ....

Action: Art bet £1500. Joe called and Fred raised £6000. Art had £15,000 left, Joe £5000, while Fred more than covered them both. The pot was £12,920 and it was £6000 to Art.

Question 6: Should Art: (a) pass (b) call (c) raise £9000 all-in?

(a) ☐	(b) ☐	(c) ☐	Points: ....
			Total: ....

Action: Art called and so Joe called all-in for his last £5,000. Thus the final pot size was £23,920.

River: Q♦-8♠-3♥-5♥-10♥. Art held K♥-Q♥, Joe held Q♠-Q♣ and Fred held 9♥-8♥.

Thus Art won a very nice pot, thank you very much. Joe slowplayed his hand into oblivion. Who could blame him? It looked as if his hand was unbeatable on the flop. Had Art bet his strong draw on the turn, then he would have been smashed out of the pot by Joe. It was unlikely Fred that would have called, and thus Art should probably pass.

In the post-mortem Joe claimed that, if Art had raised, then he would have passed the final £5000. Well, maybe, but talk is cheap. You may think Art played like a wimp, not raising the final £9000. The decision is a close one.

David asked me whether Joe played badly by not creating more action before the flop with his pair of queens. Many players like to play this way and then simply to pass if a king or an ace hits the flop. If neither appears, they then leap into action. However, it has to be a mistake if you never raise before the flop. Part of the art of poker is being unpredictable.

SCORECHART

60 You are making me jealous.

50-59 I would have scored in the region of 50-53. David scored 57, as did Joe. There were many marginal decisions here.

40-49 Danny scored 45. This is still a highly respectable score.

25-39 Probably you did not play sufficiently coherently.

10-24 It is entirely possible that you are not used to playing against opponents of such a high standard.

0-9 There is no excuse for such a poor score.

ANSWERS AND ANALYSIS

Holding: K♥-Q♥.

Answer 1: (a) -3 (b) 10 (c) 0 (d) 7.

I reckon K-Q suited is about the ninth best hold'em hand. It has excellent potential. There is a great deal to be said for just calling, since raising is a little like trying to buck City Hall. There are just so many players in the hand. If someone were then to reraise, Art should definitely pass. On the other hand, just calling may be giving a free flop to several much weaker hands.

Flop: Q♦-8♠-3♥.

Answer 2: (a) 1 (b) 0 (c) 10.

This is a pretty good hand. It would be a pity to give free cards.

Answer 3: (a) 10 (b) 1 (c) -2 (d) -5.

Neither opponent can be on a draw. The absolute minimum that Joe and Fred can realistically hold is A-Q. Nothing much has been lost by being taken off this hand. Art has only five improving cards, and none of them may be adequate to take the lead.

Turn: Q♦-8♠-3♥-5♥.

Answer 4: (a) 10 (b) 2 (c) 4.

Art now has an enormous drawing hand, and he does not want to risk being taken off it. If he is still winning, which seems unlikely given that he was called in two spots on the flop, it is going to be very hard to outdraw him. It is much the best play not to rock the boat.

River: Q♦-8♠-3♥-5♥-10♥.

Answer 5: (a) 0 (b) 2 (c) 10 (d) 8.

Art has made a monster. There is much to be said for betting less than the pot, begging for a call. From the point of view of the other two players, this may look like he is simply trying to steal the pot.

Answer 6: (a) 0 (b) 10 (c) 7.

It is logically possible for Art to be losing. Fred may have A♥-8♥, having called on the flop with a pair of eights and made a backdoor flush. If Art were to raise then Joe may not call the last bet with whatever hand he has made. This has developed into an enormous pot late in the evening. All three players were winning heavily, but now two will be shattered. Even if Art loses the hand, he will go home a winner, so there is no need to go to the table here. This would be particularly true had the hand been played in a tournament. Why should Art risk going broke?

Hand 26

The Luck of the Irish

INTRODUCTION

Let us turn to the game of Irish, which is a variant of hold'em. Here each player is dealt, say four cards and there is a betting interval. The three-card flop is then displayed face up, followed by another round of betting. At the end of this, each player discards two cards, thus reducing the game to normal two-card hold'em. After the turn there is another betting interval, and then of course the final round of betting after the river card.

It should be immediately obvious that each player's holding is much stronger than in hold'em. If you start with four cards in sequence, then it is much more likely that you will flop a straight. Thus K-Q-J-10 (or a one-gap hand such as K-Q-J-9) has a very good chance of flopping a straight. However, if you only flop four to the straight, then you are *less* likely to hit the straight with such a holding. Take this example: you hold K-Q-J-9 and the flop is 10♠-9♥-4♦. Here you have only seven nut outs (four eights and the three remaining kings).

The antes in this game were £25-£25. Two people had called and most of the other players had passed. I held Q♠-Q♥-8♠-8♦ in late position. The pot was £100 and it was £25 to me.

THE PLAY

Question 1: Should I: (a) pass (b) call (c) raise £25 (d) raise £125?

(a) ☐	(b) ☐	(c) ☐	(d) ☐	Points: ....

Action: Well, you know me. I raised £125. Only one player called, The Politician, whom you may have met in my Omaha book. Rather unusually for this game, I had at least succeeded in slimming down the field.

Flop: Q♦-J♠-10♦. I held Q♠-Q♥-8♠-8♦. The pot stood at £375 and The Politician checked to me.

Question 2: Should I: (a) check (b) bet £125 (c) bet £375?

(a) ☐	(b) ☐	(c) ☐	Points: ....

Action: I bet £350 and The Politician called. The pot now stood at £1075.

Question 3: Which two cards should I retain: (a) Q♠-Q♥ (b) Q♠-8♠ (c) 8♠-8♦?

(a) ☐	(b) ☐	(c) ☐	Points: ....

Action: I retained the two queens.

Turn: Q♦-J♠-10♦-A♣. I held Q♠-Q♥. Now The Politician bet £500. There was £1575 in the pot and it was £500 to me.

Question 4: Should I: (a) pass (b) call (c) raise £500 (d) raise £2000?

(a) ☐	(b) ☐	(c) ☐	(d) ☐	Points: ....

Hypothetical River: Q♦-J♠-10♦-A♣-10♠. I hold Q♠-Q♥. The Politician checks.

Question 5: Should I: (a) check (b) bet £500 (c) bet £2075?

(a) ☐	(b) ☐	(c) ☐	Points: ....

Question 6: Facing a full £2075 bet, should The Politician: (a) pass (b) call (c) raise £2075 (d) raise £6000?

(a) ☐	(b) ☐	(c) ☐	(d) ☐	Points: ....

Another Hypothetical River: Q♦-J♠-10♦-A♣-3♦. I hold Q♠-Q♥ and the pot stands at £2075. The Politician now checks.

Question 7: Should I: (a) check (b) £500 (c) bet £2075?

(a) ☐	(b) ☐	(c) ☐	Points: ....

Let us return to the actual hand.

River: Q♦-J♠-10♦-A♣-3♠. I held Q♠-Q♥. The Politician now bet £25, bringing the pot up to £2100.

Question 8: Should I: (a) pass (b) call (c) raise £25 (d) raise £500 (e) raise £2000?

(a) ☐	(b) ☐	(c) ☐	(d) ☐	(e) ☐	Points: ....
					Total: ....

Action: I passed and The Politician nearly fell off his chair. This hand made *The Independent* newspaper. I was quoted as saying, '£25 is £25. Why waste it?' To imagine that my pot odds of 80/1 are worth anything would be ridiculous. There is no chance at all that I was winning here.

SCORECHART

80 Excellent. If you have never played this game, you have grasped the principles admirably.

70-79 I scored 77, as did David. There was no need to raise from the off.

55-69 An acceptable performance.

40-54 Well, it is probably a new game for you.

25-39 Do not select this game when playing 'dealer's choice'.

10-24 You probably do not understand certain basic poker concepts.

0-9 Reread the chapter. Or perhaps it is a closed book to you.

ANSWERS AND ANALYSIS

Holding: Q♠-Q♥-8♠-8♦.

Answer 1: (a) 0 (b) 10 (c) 3 (d) 7.

There is no really good hand in this game, just good flops. Of course, having a pair of aces and a nut flush draw is always attractive, while being last to act is, as usual, highly desirable.

Flop: Q♦-J♠-10♦.

Answer 2: (a) 7 (b) 0 (c) 10.

The nut trips is a very fair hand. Betting here, and thus pretending that I have A-K, is a perfectly acceptable play. The Politician seldom raises on the flop, but even if he does, I am less than 2/1 against making a full house by the river.

Answer 3: (a) 10 (b) -5 (c) -5.

There is no putting one over on you is there? If you failed to answer (a), then you do not understand this game at all.

Turn: Q♦-J♠-10♦-A♣.

Answer 4: (a) 0 (b) 10 (c) -5 (d) -5.

Clearly The Politician has a king, which is all he needs for the nut straight. He is winning, and is obviously never going to pass a raise. He may even have a hand such as A♦-K♦, so a raise would be diabolically bad.

WARNING: Complex maths follows

If I give him A-K for his hand, then I have 9 cards with which to pair up and 3 kings with which to split the pot. We can count that as 10½ outs. I can see

4 cards on the board and my own 4 cards, but in this instance I have also 'seen' 2 of his cards. Thus I know 10 cards and there are 42 left, of which I win with 10½ and lose with 31½. I am 3/1 underdog and £1575/£500 is slightly better than 3/1. I clearly just about have my pot odds. But it is much, much better than that...

Answer 5: (a) -5 (b) -2 (c) 10.

I should bet the full pot with my big full house.

Answer 6: (a) 0 (b) 10 (c) 0 (d) 0.

From his perspective, I most likely have the straight with him. Since I only have two cards, it is impossible for me to have both a full house and the straight. In that case it would be wrong for him to pass, so I might as well wring the maximum out of this situation myself.

Thus my implied odds on the turn are tremendous: with three cards I split £1075, making a profit of £537.50, and with nine cards I make £3650 profit.

Total £34,462.50 for an outlay of £21,000. This is a profit of £321 per hand.

Answer 7: (a) 10 (b) -3 (c) -5.

The Politician thinks I must have the straight, since if I had a hand such as K♦-9♦, I would have raised on the turn. I would then be splitting the pot and freerolling with the diamonds. Indeed, The Politician may be lurking in the grass and have precisely that hand himself. Thus it would be really stupid for me to bluff here.

River: Q♦-J♠-10♦-A♣-3♠.

Answer 8: (a) 10 (b) 3 (c) 0 (d) -5 (e) -5.

There is no greater certainty than that The Politician had the nut straight.

Hand 27

You may not believe me

INTRODUCTION

This hand was again Irish, the rules of which were explained in the previous hand. It was a £1000 buy-in game, with blinds of £25-25. The encounter took place in 2002 and I was just a passive observer. You take up the hand of Ali, a player you have met before in this book (and who also appears in my Omaha book).

A player went a voluntary £50 over-blind. Mel was one of only two callers before the action came to Ali on the button. Mel had not been doing well and his money had trickled down to £600. We all know the feeling. Personally I usually prefer to add-on to avoid becoming the poor relation at the feast, although I may well wait until I have the button before I do so. Thus the pot stood at £200 and it was £50 to Ali, who held K♠-K♥-4♠-3♥.

THE PLAY

Question 1: Should Ali: (a) pass (b) call (c) raise £50 (d) raise £250?

(a) ☐	(b) ☐	(c) ☐	(d) ☐	Points: ....

Action: Ali raised £250. The other players passed and Mel raised £350 all-in, so the pot was now up to £1100.

Question 2: Should Ali: (a) pass (b) call?

(a) ☐	(b) ☐	Points: ....

Action: Ali called.

Flop: A♣-K♦-5♥. Ali held K♠-K♥-4♠-3♥. Mel threw his two extra cards away rapidly.

Question 3: Which two cards should Ali keep: (a) K♠-K♥ (b) K♠-4♠ (c) K♥-3♥ (d) 4♠-3♥?

(a) ☐	(b) ☐	(c) ☐	(d) ☐	Points: ....
				Total: ....

Action: Ali kept 4♠-3♥. I do not think I could have brought myself to make that play.

Turn: A♣-K♦-5♥-2♠. Ali held 4♠-3♥ and had now hit the front. Here Mel uttered the immortal words, 'Give me the case king.'

River: A♣-K♦-5♥-2♠-K♣. Ali held 4♠-3♥ and Mel held A♠-A♣. Thus Mel won the pot. If only Ali had not read the situation so well, he would have won with quad kings. This seems desperately sad!

Of course, the whole table erupted. Everyone gathered around to see what had happened. You would say it was ridiculous if you saw it in a film. But I was there and I will never see the likes of it again.

There seems to be something about the game of Irish that makes for peculiar situations. This presumably is one reason why The Politician likes it so much and always chooses it on his button.

SCORECHART

30 I think that you must have cheated and looked at the answer.

20-29 I scored 25. Ali made the same score by a different route. Danny and David only managed 20.

10-19 Perhaps you are just unlucky.

0-9 If you made a similar poor score for Hand 26, do not select Irish when it is your choice of game.

ANSWERS AND ANALYSIS

Holding: K♠-K♥-4♠-3♥.

Answer 1: (a) -1 (b) 10 (c) 1 (d) 5.

This is an okay hand, but nothing special. Probably Ali should have shown greater respect and just called.

Answer 2: (a) -2 (b) 10.

Ali is receiving better than 3/1 odds on his money. In the game of Irish there should be no hand where you raise, receive such odds and then pass.

Flop: A♣-K♦-5♥.

Answer 3: (a) 5 (b) -5 (c) 0 (d) 10.

Ali actually showed his hand and said that Mel must have aces. Thus he discarded his trip kings and kept his small straight draw. As Ali saw it, he was 20/1 against making quad kings, but only 5/1 against making the straight. In the spirit of the game, Mel demonstrated that he did indeed hold aces.

Hand 28

Bread and Butter

INTRODUCTION

It is a standard pot-limit £500 buy-in game with £10-£20 blinds. I was in the big blind with 7♥-4♦. Three players had called and the small blind had passed. The pot stood at £90.

THE PLAY

Question 1: Should I: (a) check (b) bet £20 (c) bet £90?

(a) ☐	(b) ☐	(c) ☐	Points: ....

Action: I checked.

Flop: 9♠-5♦-2♣. I held 7♥-4♦. The pot was £90.

Question 2: Should I: (a) check (b) bet £25 (c) bet £90?

(a) ☐	(b) ☐	(c) ☐	Points: ....

Action: I checked and all three opponents followed along like lambs.

Turn: 9♠-5♦-2♣-5♥. I held 7♥-4♦. The pot was still £90.

Question 3: Should I: (a) check (b) bet £25 (c) bet £90?

(a) ☐	(b) ☐	(c) ☐	Points: ....

Action: I bet £75 and everyone passed. I muttered the usual platitudes as I gathered up my table charges for the rest of the evening, 'It's a dirty job, but somebody's got to do it.' After all these years, perhaps it is a case of inbreeding, but my hand gravitates to the chips and makes such bluffs of its own volition.

Hypothetical Action: Instead of folding, Joe calls me and both other players pass.

Hypothetical River: 9♠-5♦-2♣-5♥-8♦. I hold 7♥-4♦. The pot stands at £270.

Question 4: Should I: (a) check (b) bet £75 (c) bet £200?

(a) ☐	(b) ☐	(c) ☐	Points: ....

Action: I check and Joe checks. I proudly show my hand. Joe now asks, 'What's that?' He is told it is 9♠-8♦-7♥-5♦-5♥. In triumph he shows down his A♣-J♦ and says, 'I thought you were on a steal.' Yes, well. My small bluff has improved my image as the last of the big spenders!

Let us take a look at a different river scenario.

Hypothetical River: 9♠-5♦-2♣-5♥-4♠. I held 7♥-4♦. The pot stands at £270.

Question 5: Should I: (a) check (b) bet £75 (c) bet £200?

(a) ☐	(b) ☐	(c) ☐	Points: ....
			Total: ....

Action: I check and once again Joe checks. I show my pair of fours and Joe sulkily shows his A-J and says, 'I thought you were bluffing.' He whinges for a bit and then raises on some marginal hands to the detriment of his bank balance, but does not go on tilt.

SCORECHART

50 Matching my score. You are playing impeccable poker.

40-49 Perfectly respectable. David made 43.

25-39 Perhaps you thought there was a catch and adjusted your play accordingly. Are you trying to play poker against a book? I suppose that's not a bad idea! Danny scored 30.

10-24 A feeble score.

2-9 Go to the bottom of the class.

ANSWERS AND ANALYSIS

Holding: 7♥-4♦.

Answer 1: (a) 10 (b) 0 (c) 2.

My hand is nothing to write home about. All three limpers must have better hands than me. Some may be very strong and lurking in the bushes, so this is not the time to start bluffing.

Flop: 9♠-5♦-2♣.

Answer 2: (a) 10 (b) 0 (c) 1.

With three limpers in the pot it is entirely possible that someone has made a pair of nines. There is no reason to get brave.

Turn: 9♠-5♦-2♣-5♥.

Answer 3: (a) 8 (b) 0 (c) 10.

Nobody has shown any interest. The money seems to be just lying around waiting to be picked up. From the viewpoint of my supine opponents, I may have absolutely anything, including a five in my hand, since I was the forced blind.

Answer 4: (a) 10 (b) 0 (c) 5.

That's enough. I've pushed out the boat as far as I want to, and should give in gracefully.

Answer 5: (a) 10 (b) 2 (c) 5.

I have no reason to rock the boat, but I have finally made a little something. Just as when I hit a blank, it is best to go passive.

Hand 29

Relax yourself

INTRODUCTION

This hand arose in another £10-£20 blind game. Before it came to me Terry had limped in and Joe had raised £70. Thus the pot stood at £140 and it was £90 to me. Everyone had plenty of money left. I was seventh in hand with Q♠-Q♦.

THE PLAY

Question 1: Should I: (a) pass (b) call (c) raise £90 (d) raise £230?

(a) ☐	(b) ☐	(c) ☐	(d) ☐	Points: ....

Action: I called and everyone else passed, including Terry. Mission accomplished, I am alone with Joe, at little risk to my stack so far.

Hypothetical Flop: K♥-7♠-3♦. I hold Q♠-Q♦ and the pot stands at £230. Joe bets £200, bringing the pot up to £430.

Question 2: Should I: (a) pass (b) call (c) raise £200 (d) raise £630?

(a) ☐	(b) ☐	(c) ☐	(d) ☐	Points: ....

Flop: 9♦-7♠-3♦. I held Q♠-Q♦. Joe bet £200, so the pot went from £230 to £430.

Question 3: Should I: (a) pass (b) call (c) raise £200 (d) raise £630?

(a) ☐	(b) ☐	(c) ☐	(d) ☐	Points: ....

Action: I raised £600 and Joe called. At this stage I had £5000 left and Joe had me covered.

Turn: 9♦-7♠-3♦-2♣. I held Q♠-Q♦. The pot stood at £1830 and Joe checked.

Question 4: Should I: (a) check (b) bet £600 (c) bet £1800.

(a) ☐	(b) ☐	(c) ☐	Points: ....

Action: I bet £1600 to allow him to think that I am a little anxious about being called. The only drawing hand with pot odds is A♦-K♦, but he would probably have reraised with that on the flop. What if he does raise here? Well, I will just have to deal with that problem if and when it arises. In actual fact, Joe just called.

River: 9♦-7♠-3♦-4♣-3♥. I held Q♠-Q♦. The pot stood at £5030 and I had £3400 left. Joe checked.

Question 5/1: In a *tournament*, should I: (a) check (b) bet £1600 (c) bet £3400 all-in?

(a) ☐ (b) ☐ (c) ☐ Points: ....

Question 5/2: In a *cash game*, should I: (a) check (b) bet £1600 (c) bet £3400 all-in?

(a) ☐ (b) ☐ (c) ☐ Points: ....

Action: I went all-in. Joe called with J♠-J♥.

I showed my winning hand and Joe said, 'I didn't think you would slowplay queens before the flop.' I smiled to myself and thought, 'That is not what I considered the call to be.'

Question 6: Did Joe play badly: (a) no (b) maybe (c) yes?

(a) ☐ (b) ☐ (c) ☐ Points: ....

Total: ....

SCORECHART

70 Better than I could manage. Yet this was Danny's score.

60-69 A very fine result indeed. I made 64 and I created the scoring system! David made 66.

45-59 I hope that you did not get into a muddle.

30-44 Reread this chapter.

15-29 Indeed, reread the whole book. David Sklansky recommends you go back over his material at regular intervals.

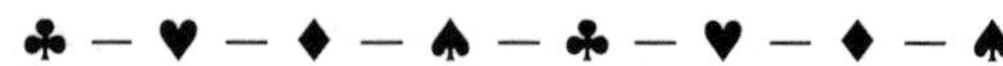

ANSWERS AND ANALYSIS

Holding: Q♠-Q♦.

Answer 1: (a) -1 (b) 10 (c) 2 (d) 4.

It really doesn't matter whether this is a cash game, a tournament, pot- limit or no-limit. The hand can be played the same way.

The gap concept tells us that Joe should have raised with a somewhat better hand than if there had been no intervention by Terry. Extended gap theory says that I should call with a considerably better hand than that with which I would have raised, had no-one else entered the pot yet.

Do you fancy trying to quantify the situation, just as if you were a computer? If not, you should skip the next five paragraphs.

WARNING: Complex maths follows

Terry should be calling with a holding in the top 50% of all hands. I have no idea how to work out, at the table, what that means when there are still so many people left to act. I will have to leave that to mathematicians or computers.

It costs Joe £20 to call to win a pot of £50. Assuming we ignore implied odds, he needs his hand to be in the top 60% of what he imagines Terry to hold, itself the best 50%.

Thus he should enter into contention with the top 30% and should raise with the top 15%. His gap has already been extended. Dr Mahmood Mahmood tells me the minimum holding needed is 9-9 when there are seven players still in play. Where does he get this from?

I rate 9-9 in the top 10% of all hands. The probability 9-9 is the best hand is:

90% if there is one opponent.

90 x 0.9 = 81% if there are two opponents.

90 x 0.9 x 0.9 = 72.9% if there are three opponents.

90 x 0.9 x 0.9 x 0.9 = 65.6% if there are four opponents.

90 x 0.9 x 0.9 x 0.9 x 0.9 = 59% if there are five opponents.

90 x 0.9 x 0.9 x 0.9 x 0.9 x 0.9 = 53.1% if there are six opponents.

90 x 0.9 x 0.9 x 0.9 x 0.9 x 0.9 x 0.9 = 47.8% if there are seven opponents.

Thus 9-9 is the watershed hand that defines whether we should raise when there are six to seven opponents in a hand who have taken little positive action. This again points to the advantage of late position. The fewer players in the pot, the weaker the hand you need with which to raise.

In the actual hand it will cost me £90 to call to win a pot of £140. Thus I should pass unless my hand is in the top 50/140 x 15% = 5% approximately.

I can only consider raising with the top 2½% of hands. The extended gap has taken my action from the top 50% to 2½% due to the betting of two players.

It is impossible to overestimate the value of position in such cases. I should only raise with A-A, K-K, Q-Q or A-K.

Returning to playing poker: If I raise, then I am only going to be called, or reraised by pocket aces, pocket kings or possibly A-K. Against the latter I am only a small favourite, and A-K is only 33% more likely than either of the first two hands. Raising propels me into an unhealthy situation, since I will only be challenged either by a much stronger hand than mine, or one that is a small underdog. In addition, if I am reraised, I will have to pass and lose my implied odds of making a killing if a queen were to come on the flop. The advantage of raising is that I am chasing off inferior hands, plus probably the other pair of queens. However, I am willing to forego that in view of the risks involved.

Is there any form of poker in which player with pocket queens should make the second raise? There certainly is. In limit hold'em it would be sub-optimal not to do so. Also, in a one-table no-limit satellite, this may be the best hand you will see. In that case, closing your eyes and raising all-in is a perfectly sound strategy. However, please do not do so literally, since that may be interpreted as a tell. In addition, satellites are often played fast and loose, so you may actually be way ahead of the field with your pair of queens.

Answer 2: (a) 10 (b) 2 (c) 4 (d) 0.

Joe may well be over-betting his hand. However, if the king is a danger card to him, he will often check. By playing rather passively, and now passing, I have eliminated the danger of being destroyed by A-K, albeit at the cost of losing a pot I might otherwise have won. This play is particularly effective in a long tournament, where you haven't amassed many chips and survival is paramount.

Making a small gay raise here has some merit. Joe may well capitulate, but if not, then I can always kiss goodbye to my £400 investment.

Flop: 9♦-7♠-3♦.

Answer 3: (a) 0 (b) 6 (c) 2 (d) 10.

I have learnt very little about Joe's hand, since he should bet here whatever his holding. Indeed, I might be more wary of a check. Realistically, there are only two hands that I need be afraid of: pocket aces and pocket kings. The mere act of calling tells Joe I am interested in the pot, whereas a small raise might allow him adequate implied odds with a hand such as A-K or X-9 or 10♦-8♦. Indeed, from his perspective, once I raise he has to consider that either of the latter two could actually be my hand. Empathising with your opponent's viewpoint is a very important skill in poker. I do not want to allow him in cheap, only to find that an ace or king hits on the turn. A strong raise is best.

Turn: 9♦-7♠-3♦-2♣.

Answer 4: (a) 0 (b) 2 (c) 10.

It is very unlikely that the 2♣ has made any difference. Are you a man or a mouse? You are probably winning and either want to extract more or get Joe to pass. He is not drawing dead. Thus the only reason for checking here is if you think Joe is going to pass a turn bet but will bluff on the river, if you allow him to.

Gap theory can help even in this complex situation. What does Joe hold: trips, aces, kings, queens, jacks, tens, A♦-X♦ or A-K (believing me to be on a draw)? It seems unlikely that such an experienced player would raise before the flop with 9-9, 7-7, 3-3 (or A♦-7♦) with so many players still to act after him. After just calling my flop raise, Joe has now checked, so his hand is likely to be weaker than trips. Thus the only two hands that I need really fear are A-A or K-K, but even those seem unlikely given his flop and turn play.

River: 9♦-7♠-3♦-4♣-3♥.

Answer 5/1: (a) 10 (b) 0 (c) 2.

Answer 5/2: (a) 10 (b) 0 (c) 6.

This is a pure poker decision. What is the likelihood of Joe calling with a hand worse than mine or passing with a hand that is superior? Can I perhaps get him to lay down Q♥-Q♣? You have to know Joe to decide that.

In a tournament, where you are staking your life's blood, a check is much more circumspect. I trust that you would not be playing with money you cannot afford to lose in a cash game.

You may be able to make a small bet of £1600, but I would not know whether I was coming or going were Joe then to raise £1800 all-in.

Answer 6: (a) 2 (b) 8 (c) 10.

I could well have had A♦-7♦ or 10♦-8♦. One possibility would be for him to reraise me on the flop. Since I would have no reason to read *him* for either of those hands, I might possibly decide to pass, although I could actually beat his jacks. If instead I were to reraise again, then he could pass unless he reads me for a drawing hand.

Another alternative is for him to come out betting on the turn. Say he bets £1500. It would be very odd if I were to raise £3500 all-in here with a drawing hand, so he can just swallow it and pass if I raise. It is perfectly feasible for me to have trips.

In either case, he would put the pressure back on me, while the cost at the end of the day would have either been the same or less. The initiative is always important – that is why the right to fire the first shot can sometimes outweigh the advantage of acting last.

Could Joe have used the extended gap concept to pass at any stage? He can assume I raised on the flop with A♦-X♦, 10♦-8♦, a nine, a pair of tens or better, or a pure bluff. He can call provided his hand is within the top 67% of this lot. Clearly that is so.

We move to the turn. We listed his possible hands earlier. Presumably I would only bet out with a drawing hand, or a pair of tens or better. Jacks are not high on that list and a pass is in order here.

I have chosen to bet yet again on the river. Surely the likelihood of his winning is now too low to justify a call? Has Joe not fallen into the error of calling with virtually the weakest hand with which I could conceivably be betting?

We are often exhorted to avoid calling with a hand that can only beat a bluff. However, the principle of passing a made hand with only a low percentage probability of winning, has seldom been remarked upon in the literature.

Hand 30

Where was he?

INTRODUCTION

In this game the blinds were £25-£50. Two players had called prior to Bill and there were still two others to act. Bill held 9♥-9♦. There was £175 in the pot and it was £50 to him.

THE PLAY

Question 1: Should Bill: (a) pass (b) call (c) raise £50 (d) raise £225?

(a) ☐	(b) ☐	(c) ☐	(d) ☐	Points: ....

Action: Bill called. A player after him called, as did the small blind, while the big blind took no further action. There were therefore six players for the flop.

Flop: J♥-10♠-8♥. Bill held 9♥-9♦. The pot stood at £300. The first four players all checked, so the action was now on Bill.

Question 2: Should Bill: (a) check (b) bet £50 (c) bet £300?

(a) ☐	(b) ☐	(c) ☐	Points: ....

Action: Bill checked, as did the fifth opponent in the pot.

Turn: J♥-10♠-8♥-9♣. Bill held 9♥-9♦. The pot was still £300. All four players again checked to Bill. Remember that there was still one opponent to follow.

Question 3: Should Bill: (a) check (b) bet £50 (c) bet £300?

(a) ☐	(b) ☐	(c) ☐	Points: ....

Action: Bill checked. Finally the only other person left to speak, Fred, sprang to life with a £250 bet. Craig, in the small blind, called, and all the other players made their excuses and left. The pot stood at £800 and it was £250 to go to Bill.

Question 4: Should Bill: (a) pass (b) call (c) raise £250 (d) raise £1050?

(a) ☐	(b) ☐	(c) ☐	(d) ☐	Points: ....

River: J♥-10♠-8♥-9♣-J♦. Bill held 9♥-9♦ with £1050 in the pot. Craig bet £1000. All three players were caked up and the pot was now £2050.

Question 5: Should Bill: (a) pass (b) call (c) raise £1000 (d) raise £3000?

(a) ☐	(b) ☐	(c) ☐	(d) ☐	Points: ....
				Total: ....

Action: Bill called. Fred studied the board for a long time, heaved a deep sigh, and passed. Craig then turned over J♠-8♦.

Bill muttered, 'Jammy so and so,' under his breath. He had felt all at sea throughout the pot. At least it wasn't a gigantic loss. And then, once again it was 'shuffle up and deal'.

SCORECHART

50 I steeled myself and scraped full marks. The temptation to bet at some stage is enormous.

40-49 You showed excellent self-control for most of the hand.

25-39 Very respectable. Danny scored 32.

10-24 An unacceptable score. Let us hope you have learnt your lesson well, at only the cost of this book.

0-9 Back to the drawing board.

ANSWERS AND ANALYSIS

Holding: 9♥-9♦.

Answer 1: (a) 0 (b) 10 (c) 1 (d) 4.

This is not a bad hand, but the last thing he wants to do here is manufacture a crisis. Bill has good position and potentially a very good, albeit unlikely, drawing hand. The correct decision must be just to call.

Flop: J♥-10♠-8♥.

Answer 2: (a) 10 (b) -3 (c) 2.

This is another one of those hands where you do not mind being called if you bet, but you would bitterly resent being raised. It would be nice to thin down the field to one opponent, since then a seven or queen would most likely be enough for him to win. However, because there was no pre-flop raise, all things are possible. Someone else may have a nine in the hole and possibly could even have flopped a straight.

Turn: J♥-10♠-8♥-9♣.

Answer 3: (a) 10 (b) 0 (c) 4.

All anybody has to have is a queen or seven in the hole to be beating Bill. The only possible justification for a bet is that, if he fills up, he may be well paid. The downside of checking is that if he is actually winning, then there are still many ways he could be outdrawn by someone taking a free card. It is frustrating to have to check with trips, but necessary in this case.

Answer 4: (a) 2 (b) 10 (c) 0 (d) 0.

I am not going to suggest that you pass trips with one card to come in hold'em for such a small bet. You are not going to do it. But please, please do not raise and expose yourself to a reraise. Remember, it is possible that all three of you may split the pot if a queen comes on the river.

River: J♥-10♠-8♥-9♣-J♦.

Answer 5: (a) 2 (b) 10 (c) 2 (d) 0.

Craig has made no effort to bet at any stage. But he did call on the turn and now launches into action. Can he have made a higher full house? We would be used to that at pot-limit Omaha and might well pass in such a situation. Here a flat call may encourage Fred to call with a queen. Escalating the pot is neither necessary, nor technically sound.

Hand 31

Loose

INTRODUCTION

The game was £10-£20 blinds. Hal had made it £80 to go in seat 3 and two players had called. Jill held Q♥-J♦ and was sitting in trap 7, so there were two other players who were yet to act. The pot was up to £270 and it was £80 to Jill.

THE PLAY

Question 1: Should Jill: (a) pass (b) call (c) raise £80 (d) raise £350?

(a) ☐	(b) ☐	(c) ☐	(d) ☐	Points: ....

Action: You will not be surprised to learn that Jill called. Well, otherwise there would be no story! The two remaining players and both blinds now passed. First phase – 'Mission accomplished'. Jill has secured the button and reached the flop without further incident.

Flop: 9♠-8♦-4♣. Jill held Q♥-J♦ and there was £350 in the pot. Hal now bet £250, which was called by both Nick and Ralph, bringing the pot up to £1100.

Question 2: Should Jill: (a) pass (b) call (c) raise £250 (d) raise £1350?

(a) ☐	(b) ☐	(c) ☐	(d) ☐	Points: ....

Action: Jill called £250.

Turn: 9♠-8♦-4♣-10♥. Jill held Q♥-J♦ and the pot was £1350. Hal bet £1350, leaving himself with a further £6000, and Nick raised £2000 all-in. Ralph then passed. The pot stood at £6050 and it was £3350 to Jill.

Question 3: Should Jill: (a) pass (b) call (c) raise £4000 all-in?

(a) ☐	(b) ☐	(c) ☐	Points: ....

Action: Jill called £3350 and Hal also called. The pot stood at £11,400.

River: 9♠-8♦-4♣-10♥-5♥. Jill held Q♥-J♦. Hal checked.

Question 4: Should Jill: (a) check (b) bet £2000 (c) bet £4000 all-in?

(a) ☐ (b) ☐ (c) ☐ Points: ....

Action: Jill bet £2000. Hal sat for ages and finally called. It turned out that Nick had 7♠-6♠. He only had the ignorant end of the straight draw on the flop. That is, only a five would have given him the nuts. Calling to make such a hand can be fraught with difficulties, even in hold'em. Even so, it was a much better hand on the flop than Jill's hand.

Hal had 9♥-9♦ for a set of nines. It is not usually Hal's style to open for a raise first in hand with a pair this low. He was really unlucky to lose so much money.

Both Nick and Hal berated Jill for playing so loosely, but she just raked in the money, saying, 'You must love playing with people like me.'

WARNING: Complex maths follows

Were they correct? Was Jill's flop play against the odds? Let us analyse the facts. Jill's flop investment was £250, in return for which she won £1100 + £1350 + £3350 + £2000 + £2000 = £9800. Her actual return proved to be £9800/£250 = 39/1.

What about Hal's possibly of a redraw on the river card? We can see four cards on the board, Hal's own pocket nines, Nick's 7♠-6♠ and Jill's Q♥-J♦. He makes a full house with ten cards out of 42. Let us suppose that he would bet the £4000 left and Jill would call. Thus her expected redraw loss would be £7600 x 10/42 = £1809.

Thus Jill's true potential profit from hitting her hand on the turn card was £9800 - £1809 = £7991 and her implied odds on the flop were therefore £7991/£250 = 32/1. She was 11/1 against making the straight. Thus we can say that, on a good day, with a following wind, against these particular players, holding those particular cards, 'Her call was totally justified.'

That is a lot of ifs and buts. Do remember that she needed position and for her opponents to have plenty of chips and rather specific cards in order to justify the play. But she hit what proved to be a true Weapon of Mass Destruction.

Hypothetical Action: As before, but Hal bets £1200 on the turn and the other two players pass. The pot is £2550. Remember that we do not know Hal's hand, so it may differ from the previous scenario.

Question 5: Should Jill: (a) pass (b) call (c) raise £1200 (d) raise £3750?

(a) ☐ (b) ☐ (c) ☐ (d) ☐ Points: ....

Hypothetical Action: Jill flat calls. The river was as before and Hal checks. The pot stands at £3750.

Question 6: Should Jill: (a) check (b) bet £1200 (c) bet £3500?

(a) ☐	(b) ☐	(c) ☐	Points: ....
			Total: ....

Action: Jill bets £1000. Hal shows his aces and passes. No variation on the play was going to get Hal to put any more money in this pot.

This time Jill has won £2300 for her £250 stake. This is 9/1 and, once again Jill receives adequate implied odds.

SCORECHART

60 Very conservative, and correct, play.

50-59 Danny scored 54 and David 52. I think that my score would have been similar. It is hard to tell.

35-49 It is easy to play this hand to score 35 points.

20-34 Really, it is only now that your score is becoming mediocre.

5-19 Not a very good sign. Reread the chapter.

0-4 To do this badly, you must surely have passed the nuts.

ANSWERS AND ANALYSIS

Holding: Q♥-J♦.

Answer 1: (a) 10 (b) 7 (c) 0 (d) 0.

It stands to reason that there are better hands out there than hers at this stage. A call would be relying mainly on the implied odds, but it is impossible to assess what she may win. Furthermore, two people have already called, and they may well have some of the cards that she is looking for. Finally, there are two late position players and the two blinds yet to act, any one of whom may be intending to raise.

Flop: 9♠-8♦-4♣.

Answer 2: (a) 10 (b) 4 (c) -2 (d) -5.

It is possible that either a jack or a queen on the turn may give Jill the winning hand. However, it is more likely to be a disaster, helping another player to make a straight. Thus realistically Jill has only four winning cards, the tens.

She can see five cards out of 52. Thus she has four wins out of 47 unseen cards, which is roughly 8½% or 11/1. However, it is possible to make the hand not only of the turn, but also the river. Therefore is not the probability

16%, which is about 5/1? Since she is getting £1100/250 or 4.4/1, that is surely good enough when you include implied odds?

No, this line of reasoning is completely fallacious. Let us imagine that the turn brings 9♠-8♦-4♣-2♣. The bet is £1000. Now Jill will have to been forced to spend a total of £1250 to reach the river. Clearly, it is impossible to imagine, by any stroke of the imagination, that Jill has adequate pot odds. The only possible justification in calling here lies in the implied odds.

Answer 3: (a) -5 (b) 6 (c) 10.

Jill is winning, but it also seems likely that she can be outdrawn. What can her opponents possibly have? The choice is between calling, and probably picking up a further £2000 from Hal, or raising, and possibly making a further £4000.

Answer 4: (a) -5 (b) 4 (c) 10.

Jill should try to wring the most out of this situation. Hal will believe that he might possibly win £15,400 for £4000, which is virtually 4/1 odds. It is therefore quite likely that he will call.

Answer 5: (a) -5 (b) 10 (c) 0 (d) 8.

Jill has position and can slowplay this hand. The alternative is to raise and hope to induce a call, or even a reraise. No book can analyse every facet of such a situation, it is a pure poker conundrum.

Answer 6: (a) -5 (b) 6 (c) 10.

Jill has to milk this situation for all she can get.

Hand 32

Aggression and Defence

INTRODUCTION

The game was £10-£20 blinds. John held J♠-J♦ second to speak after the blinds, that is to say, in fourth position. The first player had passed.

THE PLAY

Question 1: Should John: (a) pass (b) call (c) raise £20 (d) raise £60? (In this hand it is assumed that small blind had already completed the blind for the purpose of calculating the maximum pre-flop raise.)

(a) ☐	(b) ☐	(c) ☐	(d) ☐	Points: ....

Action: John made it £60 to go. This is a sort of an in-between bet. You should not do this all the time with an in-between hand, since that would give the game away. Larry called in trap 7 and Stan also called on the button. Arthur called in the small blind, but the big blind passed.

Flop: 10♦-8♠-7♥. John held J♠-J♦. There was £260 in the pot. Arthur checked.

Question 2: Should John: (a) check (b) bet £50 (c) bet £260?

(a) ☐	(b) ☐	(c) ☐	Points: ....

Hypothetical Action: John bets £200, Larry raises £400 and Stan calls. The pot stands at £1660.

Question 3: Should John: (a) pass (b) call (c) raise £400 (d) raise £2000.

(a) ☐	(b) ☐	(c) ☐	(d) ☐	Points: ....

Now back to reality.

Action: John bet £200 and Larry called. The other two players passed.

Turn: 10♦-8♠-7♥-5♦. John held J♠-J♦ and the pot was £660.

Question 4: Should John: (a) check (b) bet £200 (c) bet £660?

(a) ☐	(b) ☐	(c) ☐	Points: ....

Hypothetical Action: John bets £660 and Larry raises £1600, with £1400 left.

Question 5: Should John: (a) pass (b) call (c) raise all-in?

(a) ☐	(b) ☐	(c) ☐	Points: ....

Returning to the actual hand.

Action: John bet £500 and Larry called.

River: 10♦-8♠-7♥-5♦-2♣. John held J♠-J♦ and the pot was £1660.

Question 6: Should John: (a) check (b) bet £500 (c) bet £1660?

(a) ☐	(b) ☐	(c) ☐	Points: ....

Action: John checked and so did Larry.

Hypothetical Action: Larry bets £1600, so the pot is now £3260.

Question 7: Should John: (a) pass (b) call (c) raise all-in?

(a) ☐	(b) ☐	(c) ☐	Points: ....
			Total: ....

Returning to real life.

Action: John showed down his jacks and Larry his 10♣-9♠. Perhaps Larry should either have raised on the flop or passed on the turn, but he had a tempting draw and could even have been winning.

SCORECHART

70 An excellent score. This is how Danny, David or I would have played the hand.

60-69 Some might say that your actions were superior to mine.

45-59 There is plenty of room for choice in the way that this hand can be approached.

30-44 Excuses are now wearing a little thin. Perhaps you are having an off-day.

15-29 This is not good enough for you to be a contender.

0-14 Do join in our game at the Grosvenor Victoria Casino in London.

♣ – ♥ – ♦ – ♠ – ♣ – ♥ – ♦ – ♠

ANSWERS AND ANALYSIS

Holding: J♠-J♦.

Answer 1: (a) -1 (b) 5 (c) 7 (d) 10.

The advantage of raising the maximum is that, if somebody were to reraise, you can choose to either duck out or accept the challenge. A mere call announces your interest anyway, and it would be good to sort out some of the debris. It would be different in the early stages of a tournament, where one might even consider passing such a hand.

Flop: 10♦-8♠-7♥.

Answer 2: (a) 4 (b) 0 (c) 10.

A pair of jacks should still be winning, but if you are facing a made straight, well, then a nine may still save you on the turn. It is unlikely that anyone has 9-6 since you put some pressure on before the flop, and the chance of anyone holding J-9 is somewhat diminished by the fact that you hold two of the jacks. A token bet may give the impression that you feel you are not on safe ground. Well, that is true enough. Nobody is going to believe that you have a straight, nor even a nine, in that case.

Answer 3: (a) 10 (b) 3 (c) 0 (d) 0.

This is getting too dangerous. Extended gap theory suggests that they are both stronger than just having a nine in the hole. At least one (and quite possibly both) of them currently has better than a pair of jacks.

Turn: 10♦-8♠-7♥-5♦.

Answer 4: (a) 7 (b) 0 (c) 10.

This is getting pretty hairy. It is quite possible that Larry has a strong drawing hand, including the possibility of making a diamond flush. Again, betting a small sum seems neither here nor there in this situation.

Answer 5: (a) 10 (b) 0 (c) 6.

If you are winning, then Larry probably has a hand such as A♦-9♦. From his viewpoint (not knowing John's holding) that gives him 18 outs. Thus you must either be a small favourite or a big dog for him to raise you. By betting, you have set out your agenda: you do not intend to pass. Thus a bluff from Larry is unlikely here. Also, if Larry is semi-bluffing with a large number of outs, he may know enough to realise that it is better for him if there is still betting left on the end. If you do decide to contest the pot now, it is better to raise all-in here and be done with it. The combustion point has been passed.

Answer 6: (a) 10 (b) 0 (c) 0.

Larry was probably on a draw. He will not call a bet unless he is winning.

Answer 7: (a) 7 (b) 10 (c) -5.

This very much depends on your reading of Larry. Is he simply trying to take the pot away from you, or did he have you beaten all along and was just allowing you to dig your own grave? Raising has no tactical merit whatsoever, and merely puts more money at risk for little reward.

Hand 33

Irritating but not irrational

INTRODUCTION

This was a £10-£20 game. Three players had called £20 and the small blind could not resist the extra £10. There was £100 in the pot and Joe was in the big blind with 3♥-2♠.

THE PLAY

Question 1: Should Joe: (a) check (b) raise £20 (c) raise £100?

(a) ☐	(b) ☐	(c) ☐	Points: ....

Action: Joe checked.

Flop: A♥-5♠-4♥. Joe held 3♥-2♠. The small blind checked and the pot stood at £100.

Question 2: Should Joe: (a) check (b) bet £20 (c) bet £100?

(a) ☐	(b) ☐	(c) ☐	Points: ....

Action: Joe bet £100, and Ann, Boris and Ike all called after him.

Turn: A♥-5♠-4♥-A♣. Joe held 3♥-2♠. The pot stood at £500.

Question 3: Should Joe: (a) check (b) bet £100 (c) bet £500?

(a) ☐	(b) ☐	(c) ☐	Points: ....

Action: Joe bet £300. Understandably he was becoming nervous. However, the downside with a relatively small bet is that it gives the opponents pot odds to call.

In fact, all three opponents called.

River: A♥-5♠-4♥-A♣-5♥. Joe held 3♥-2♠. There was £1700 in the pot.

Question 4: Should Joe: (a) check (b) bet £300 (c) bet £1700?

(a) ☐	(b) ☐	(c) ☐	Points: ....

Action: Joe checked. Ann now bet £1500, Boris called and Ike also called all-in for £500.

Question 5: Should Joe: (a) pass (b) call (c) raise £1500 (d) raise £4000?

(a) ☐	(b) ☐	(c) ☐	(d) ☐	Points: ....
				Total: ....

Action: Joe passed. Ann showed down A♠-J♦, Boris held A♥-K♠ and Ike K♥-J♥.

Ike immediately explained to all of us that he had to call for value. There was £4700 in the pot and it was only £500 to call. Of course, everyone nodded sagely at this nonsense. Clearly Ike had no chance of his flush being good. Boris muttered angrily that Ann was nearly drawing dead, and yet split the pot, but he had obviously forgotten about Joe and what he thought of that dreadful 5♥. You will note that Boris played intelligently on the river. Had he raised, he would not have won any more money. Indeed, he may well have won less because then even Ike may have passed.

Thus Ann and Boris split a £5200 pot. The irritating thing for Joe was that, had either one of them made even a token raise before the flop, then he would not have a lost a penny.

SCORECHART

50 Danny, David and I all achieved this score. Others might have checked this hand in the early stages.

40-49 Some of the decisions were just a matter of opinion. This is still a very good score.

30-39 Now your play is becoming rather weak.

15-29 Very poor.

0-14 I am not sure how you could do so badly.

ANSWERS AND ANALYSIS

Holding: 3♥-2♠.

Answer 1: (a) 10 (b) -5 (c) -2.

This hand has virtually no merit. One might almost feel inclined to chuck it away, although it is a freeroll. Please don't be so silly.

Flop: A♥-5♠-4♥.

Answer 2: (a) 6 (b) 3 (c) 10.

Whenever you have the nuts, it is tempting to check or bet small, and then to move in on anyone who makes a move on the pot. This is an excellent way to win a small sum of money. The problem is that, when you check-raise, you are telegraphing a message that you have a very powerful hand. If you bet out, then you may just take down the pot with no additional profit. But when somebody decides to oppose you, then it may prove highly profitable.

Although Joe has flopped the nuts, this particular hand is liable to be out-drawn. One of the other players may still hit a flush, a higher straight or a full house.

Turn: A♥-5♠-4♥-A♣.

Answer 3: (a) 4 (b) 4 (c) 10.

Joe is still in good shape. It is unlikely that any of his opponents has made a full house, but almost certain that at least one of them has an ace in the hole.

If you checked, with the aim of raising if someone else bet, then deduct three points. You may already be drawing dead. It is much more circumspect to bet out and, if you are raised, to consider passing.

If you checked on the assumption that, although you are winning, all the energy lies with the other players, then score an extra two points.

River: A♥-5♠-4♥-A♣-5♥.

Answer 4: (a) 10 (b) -5 (c) -5.

The justification for checking here is presented in the reasons for the next answer.

Answer 5: (a) 10 (b) 0 (c) -3 (d) -5.

At least two players have an ace, giving them a full house. The other player probably has a flush. It doesn't really matter. The appearance of the 5♥ clearly destroys Joe's hand.

Hand 34

No need to go mad

INTRODUCTION

This was a £10-£20 blinds game. The players in seats 3, 4 and 5 had all passed. Bill held 10♥-10♣ in seat 6. The pot stood at £30 and it was £20 to play.

THE PLAY

Question 1: Should Bill: (a) pass (b) call (c) raise £20 (d) raise £60?

(a) ☐	(b) ☐	(c) ☐	(d) ☐	Points: ....

Action: Bill made it £80 to go.

Hypothetical Action: Seat 7 raises £180. The button calls as does the small blind. The pot stands at £880 and it is £180 to Bill. He will be able to bet a further £1800 in this pot, if he should call the £180 bet.

Question 2: Should he: (a) pass (b) call (c) raise £180 (d) raise £1060?

(a) ☐	(b) ☐	(c) ☐	(d) ☐	Points: ....

Let us return to the actual hand.

Action: Cyril called on the button and all the other players passed.

Flop: 9♠-5♦-3♣. Bill held 10♥-10♣. The pot stood at £190.

Question 3: Should Bill: (a) check (b) bet £50 (c) bet £190?

(a) ☐	(b) ☐	(c) ☐	Points: ....

Action: Bill bet £190 and Cyril called.

Turn: 9♠-5♦-3♣-Q♦. Bill held 10♥-10♣. The pot stood at £570.

Question 4: Should Bill: (a) check (b) bet £200 (c) bet £570?

(a) ☐	(b) ☐	(c) ☐	Points: ....

Hypothetical Action 1: Bill checks and Cyril bets £570. The pot stands at £1710.

Question 5: Should Bill: (a) pass (b) call (c) raise £1400 all-in?

(a) ☐	(b) ☐	(c) ☐	Points: ....

Hypothetical Action 2: Instead of checking, Bill bets £570 and Cyril raises £1400 all-in.

Question 6: Should Bill: (a) pass (b) call?

(a) ☐	(b) ☐	Points: ....

Action: Bill bet £500 and Cyril called.

River: 9♠-5♦-3♣-Q♦-A♠. Bill held 10♥-10♣. The pot stood at £1570 and there was £1400 left to bet.

Question 7: Should Bill: (a) check (b) bet £500 (c) bet £1400 all-in?

(a) ☐	(b) ☐	(c) ☐	Points: ....
			Total: ....

Action: Bill checked, as did Cyril, who showed J♥-J♣.

Bill was never really in the frame. Cyril admitted that he might well have passed an all-in bet on the river. Remember, however, that talk is cheap.

SCORECHART

70 This was Danny's and my score.

60-69 You may have played the hand better than us.

45-59 There are many ways to play marginal poker hands. David scored 50.

30-44 Stick to low-stakes poker.

15-29 Yet hold'em is easier than Omaha.

0-14 There is definitely room for some improvement.

ANSWERS AND ANALYSIS

Holding: 10♥-10♣.

Answer 1: (a) -1 (b) 3 (c) 1 (d) 10.

Three players have already passed, so it is more likely that this hand is best. Although a pair of tens is probably winning at this point, the hands that act after him have a substantial positional advantage. Furthermore, there is also the 'bunching' factor. Each time a player passes, it can be assumed that the rest of the pack is richer in high cards.

Answer 2: (a) 4 (b) 10 (c) 0 (b) 1.

The very minimum type of hand that we can expect all three opponents to hold is A-K. Bill is hoping to flop a set in order to capitalise on the substantial implied odds. It is somewhat debateable whether he really has enough chips to justify a call. Received wisdom indicates that you want 20 times the money being wagered in order to justify a hand that is purely a drawing one. The fact there are three punters in the pot is encouraging when looking for either pot or implied odds or, as in this case, both.

Flop: 9♠-5♦-3♣.

Answer 3: (a) 2 (b) 0 (c) 10.

The flop seldom connects with your hand directly. In all probability Bill has the best hand. Trap-checking is not a desirable move. If Cyril were then to bet, Bill raise and Cyril reraise, the pot will have got out of hand. Bill would have to pass and forego his small chance of hitting trip tens, a hand that would be a supernova.

Thus betting is more circumspect. Another alternative is to go totally passive and just call a bet, if any, from Cyril.

Turn: 9♠-5♦-3♣-Q♦.

Answer 4: (a) 6 (b) 0 (c) 10.

The appearance of the Q♦ (or any card above a ten) is disquieting. However, the fact that there are two diamonds on the board encourages a bet, since Cyril may now call because he has made four to a flush. With the Q♥ instead, it would be difficult to visualise a calling hand that could place Bill in any real danger of being outdrawn.

Could we have applied extended gap theory to decide whether Bill's hand is worth a bet on the turn? The answer must be 'definitely possibly'.

WARNING: Complex maths follows

Bill's flop bet suggests that his holding is in the top 50% of all hands, with two cards above a nine or better, two nines or trips. Cyril's call suggests he has a hand in the top 30% of such possibilities, which would include 7-6 (people often overlook the possibility of a double belly-buster), A-X where X is a card from A-9, top pairs, overpairs, two pairs and trips.

If Bill were to bet on the turn, this would suggest he has a hand in the top 15% of all such hands. Does a pair of tens fall into this category? I have no idea.

Answer 5: (a) 10 (b) 9 (c) 0.

Answer 6: (a) 10 (b) 0.

Checking may have induced a bluff from Cyril, or he could be betting with just a pair of nines. It is impossible to tell. When Cyril raises Bill's bet, it is much more likely that he is actually winning. Bill will probably only be able to beat a bluff at this point.

Answer 7: (a) 10 (b) 2 (c) 0.

An ace is a very scary card for both players. Extended gap theory suggests very clearly that Bill will only be called by a hand that is beating his own pair. There are no cards to come, so Cyril can no longer be calling to hit a flush or straight.

Hand 35

Don't live in a Haunted House

INTRODUCTION

We are once again in a £10-£20 game. Seats 3, 4 and 5 had all passed and Tim now called. The pot stood at £50 and it was £20 to Bill in seat 7, who was again holding 10♥-10♣.

THE PLAY

Question 1: Should Bill: (a) pass (b) call (c) raise £20 (d) raise £80?

(a) ☐	(b) ☐	(c) ☐	(d) ☐	Points: ....

Action: Bill just made a gay raise of £20. He was mindful of the previous hand just a couple of minutes ago. Could lightning really strike twice? Everyone passed around to the big blind, Alf, who called, as did Tim.

Flop: 9♦-7♥-4♣. Bill held 10♥-10♣ with £130 in the pot. Both Alf and Tim checked to Bill.

Question 2: Should Bill: (a) check (b) bet £20 (c) bet £130?

(a) ☐	(b) ☐	(c) ☐	Points: ....

Action: Bill bet £50. 'Surely this is the identical flop to last time,' Bill thought. Actually he is wrong, but it is very similar. Alf passed and Tim called.

Turn: 9♦-7♥-4♣-K♠. Bill held 10♥-10♣ and the pot was now £230. Tim checked.

Question 3: Should Bill: (a) check (b) bet £50 (c) bet £230?

(a) ☐	(b) ☐	(c) ☐	Points: ....

Hypothetical Action: Bill bets £200 and Tim raises £600.

Question 4: Should Bill: (a) pass (b) call (c) raise £600 (d) raise £1800?

(a) ☐	(b) ☐	(c) ☐	(d) ☐	Points: ....

Now back to the actual hand.

Action: Bill bet £50. He still had a hangover from the previous hand. Tim called.

River: 9♦-7♥-4♣-K♠-Q♣. Bill held 10♥-10♣ and the pot stood at £330. Tim checked again.

Question 5: Should Bill: (a) check (b) bet £50 (c) bet £330?

(a) ☐	(b) ☐	(c) ☐	Points: ....
			Total: ....

Action: Bill checked. Tim turned over J♣-9♣ and Bill had thus won a small pot. Of course, had he bet the full amount at any stage, then Tim might well have become frightened and passed.

As a result of being intimidated by the unfortunate outcome of his previous hand with a pair of tens, Bill virtually maximised the chance of his being outdrawn. You should try not to be haunted by the ghost of hands past.

Tim should not have called the first £20. He only lost £140 in the pot, but why burn up money?

SCORECHART

50 I scored 50, as did Danny and David. Did you become impatient, as I did, at Bill's pusillanimous play? Remember, he may have won more by playing this way.

40-49 Fine.

25-39 Bill scored 29. You wimp!

15-24 Rather lifeless.

0-14 Oh well, on to the next hand!

ANSWERS AND ANALYSIS

Holding: 10♥-10♣.

Answer 1: (a) -1 (b) 3 (c) 2 (d) 10.

There are now only two people to act after him. However, Tim's call suggests that his hand is in the top 50%. Bill's raise should be with a hand in the top 16%. A pair of tens is ample for this purpose.

Flop: 9♦-7♥-4♣.

Answer 2: (a) 0 (b) 1 (c) 10.

Both opponents have checked, so there is no reason to think that the flop has hit them.

Turn: 9♦-7♥-4♣-K♠.

Answer 3: (a) 0 (b) 3 (c) 10.

Bill still reckons to have the best of it.

Answer 4: (a) 10 (b) 1 (c) 0 (d) -5.

Tim has come on very strong here. A check-raise is almost always a sign of strength. Perhaps he has made trips, hit a king, or holds pocket aces.

River: 9♦-7♥-4♣-K♠-Q♣.

Answer 5: (a) 10 (b) 3 (c) 3.

It is too easy for Tim to be winning. Presumably he would only call with a better hand than Bill's or a nine in the hole, if then.

Hand 36

Bluffing can be fun, but only sometimes

INTRODUCTION

Once more we are playing with blinds of £10-£20. Tony had called fourth in hand, as had Larry in fifth position, while the next three players had all passed. Ted was on the button with A♣-J♠. There was £70 in the pot and it was £20 to go.

THE PLAY

Question 1: Should Ted: (a) pass (b) call (c) raise £20 (d) raise £100?

(a) ☐	(b) ☐	(c) ☐	(d) ☐	Points: ....

Action: Ted made it £100 to go. Both blinds passed and both Tony and Larry called.

Flop: Q♣-9♣-6♣. Ted held A♣-J♠ and the pot stood at £330. Tony checked and Larry bet £300. There was now £630 in the pot and Larry had £1400 left.

Question 2: Should Ted: (a) pass (b) call (c) raise £300 (d) raise £930?

(a) ☐	(b) ☐	(c) ☐	(d) ☐	Points: ....

Action: Ted called and Tony passed.

Turn: Q♣-9♣-6♣-8♠. Ted held A♣-J♠ and the pot was now £930. Larry now checked. You will recall that he still had £1400 left on the table.

Question 3: Should Ted: (a) check (b) bet £300 (c) bet £900?

(a) ☐	(b) ☐	(c) ☐	Points: ....

Action: Ted bet £900 and Larry raised £500 all-in. Ouch! The pot stood at £3230.

Question 4: Should Ted: (a) pass (b) call?

(a) ☐	(b) ☐	Points: ....

Action: Ted called.

River: Q♣-9♣-6♣-8♠-5♥. Ted held A♣-J♠ and Larry had J♣-10♣. Thus Larry won a nice pot with his flush.

Question 5: Had Ted been able to see Larry's hand, should he have called the final bet: (a) no (b) yes?

(a) ☐ (b) ☐ Points: ....

Total: ....

SCORECHART

50 Well done. I suspect that I might have scored only 44 by calling on the flop, since I might well have missed the significance of the straight flush draw.

40-49 Danny scored 44. Well, it's an imperfect world.

30-39 Miserably as Ted played, he still scored 36. David only achieved 38.

15-29 I hope you have had better results in other hands.

1-14 You would be very welcome in our game.

ANSWERS AND ANALYSIS

Holding: A♣-J♠.

Answer 1: (a) 0 (b) 4 (c) 6 (d) 10.

This is a fairly good hand with perfect position. Players who call before the flop usually have drawing hands, or sometimes monsters. Let's find out which. Also, it is always good to shake off the tourists.

Flop: Q♣-9♣-6♣.

Answer 2: (a) 10 (b) 4 (c) 0 (d) -1.

Ted has the perfect bluffing hand, but a raise is questionable. Would he really raise if he was holding the nut flush in this position? It would be a highly unorthodox play, albeit quite a deceptive one.

Having bet, Larry has surely staked out his position; he does not intend to pass on the flop. Thus it makes more sense to call and try to take the pot away from Larry on the turn. Also, what about the chances of actually making the nut flush? Ted can see five cards, and there are 47 unknown. He has nine clubs with which to make a flush, so the odds against doing so on the next card are (47-9)/9, which is about 4/1, while he has a slightly better than 2/1 chance of making his flush by the river.

However, Larry must almost certainly have a good hand to have bet into this board, either a flush or trips. He cannot be waltzing around empty-handed. If

Larry does have a made flush then there are two fewer cards for Ted to make his hand. Furthermore, Ted's implied odds if a club comes on the turn are not very good. He is very unlikely to get paid off. Overall it would be significantly better to pass.

Turn: Q♣-9♣-6♣-8♠.

Answer 3: (a) 10 (b) 0 (c) 2.

It is certainly reasonable for Ted to bet here, acting as if he has the nut flush. If he is called, he can still make the nuts. On the other hand, by checking, he may get there at no risk whatsoever.

Answer 4: (a) 2 (b) 10.

Let us assume that Larry has a club flush. We can therefore 'see' two of his cards, in addition to the two in our hand and the four on the board, so there are now 44 unseen cards. If Larry has the flush, then Ted can win with seven cards out of these 44. His odds are therefore (44-7)/7 = 5.3/1, and he is getting money odds of £3230/£500 = 6.5/1.

River: Q♣-9♣-6♣-8♠-5♥.

Answer 5: (a) 10 (b) 0.

Ted actually only had only five outs, since the K♣ and 8♣ would have given Larry a straight flush. He was, in fact, nearly 8/1 against winning the hand. In real life, it is tough to make such fine-tuned assumptions. By making an unsuccessful bluff on the turn, Ted forced himself into a bad all-in coup.

Ted really brought this upon himself. He should have noticed the possibility of a straight flush on the flop. Since Larry called Ted's raise before the flop, he must have two decent cards, which might also be K♣-10♣ or 8♣-7♣. Perhaps Ted was confused by the fact that his opponent bet out on the flop with a made flush.

Hand 37

Telling the Story

INTRODUCTION

The blinds were $10-$20 in this game, which took place in Las Vegas. Seats 3 and 4 had passed, Howard then made it $80 to go and Arias called in seat 7. I was in seat 8 and held A♥-A♣. The pot stood at $190 and it was $80 to call.

THE PLAY

Question 1: Should I: (a) pass (b) call (c) raise $80 (d) raise $270?

(a) ☐	(b) ☐	(c) ☐	(d) ☐	Points: ....

Action: I raised $225. Everyone passed around to Howard, who called. Arias then jettisoned his holding.

Flop: 10♦-5♣-3♠. I held A♥-A♣. The pot stood at $720. Howard checked.

Question 2: Should I: (a) check (b) bet $300 (c) bet $700?

(a) ☐	(b) ☐	(c) ☐	Points: ....

Action: I bet $600 and Howard called.

Turn: 10♦-5♣-3♠-6♦. I held A♥-A♣ with $1920 in the pot. Howard checked.

Question 3: Should I: (a) check (b) bet $600 (c) bet $1900?

(a) ☐	(b) ☐	(c) ☐	Points: ....

Action: I bet $1500 and Howard called.

River: 10♦-5♣-3♠-6♦-J♥. I held A♥-A♣ and the pot was now up to $4920. Howard, who still had $4000 left, now checked. As he did so, he turned to the cocktail waitress and ordered a coffee.

Question 4: Should I: (a) check (b) bet $1500 (c) bet $4000 all-in?

(a) ☐	(b) ☐	(c) ☐	Points: ....
			Total: ....

Action: I checked. Howard now grimaced and showed down J♠-J♦. He had outdrawn me.

In some ways the idea of not betting the river when your opponent will not call unless he has a better hand, is a more important facet of a limit game that pot-limit. Saving one or two big bets at the end can make a significance difference to your profit in the long run.

SCORECHART

40 This was what Danny, David and I all scored. But David had the advantage of having just read Caro's book. Of course, I still lost quite heavily in the hand!

30-39 Highly satisfactory.

20-29 Most likely you soft-played this hand. Shame on you.

10-19 You probably played with all the aggression of a month-old lettuce.

0-9 Have you learnt nothing?

ANSWERS AND ANALYSIS

Holding: A♥-A♣.

Answer 1: (a) -5 (b) 4 (c) 5 (d) 10.

This pot is already quite active. Two players have shown considerable interest and there are still three more yet to respond. Making a small raise would be a very confusing ploy for your opponents, but it might lead them to believe you had the nuts. Anyway, Howard is often reluctant to pass, so he is likely to give action on a full-blooded raise.

Flop: 10♦-5♣-3♠.

Answer 2: (a) 0 (b) 3 (c) 10.

This pot is going smoothly. However, it would be terribly dangerous to give a free card. It is always possible to be outdrawn.

Turn: 10♦-5♣-3♠-6♦.

Answer 3: (a) 0 (b) 3 (c) 10.

Howard is much too loose a player for me to be worried about having the losing hand at this stage. A small bet seems very silly. Were he then to raise, I would not know where I stood. If I were then to pass, I would lose my shot at making trip aces. It is conceivable that he could have picked up a flush draw, so letting him in free is unwarranted.

River: 10♦-5♣-3♠-6♦-J♥.

Answer 4: (a) 10 (b) 2 (c) 0.

This is one of the best tells in the business. Mike Caro's *Book of Tells* emphasises the theme that weak means strong and strong means weak. This is much less true in England than in Vegas. Almost invariably, however, it means one of two things. Either Howard is indeed uninterested in the pot, or he is suddenly very strong. Either way, it is not worth betting here, since there is little chance of being called unless I am losing.

Hand 38

Frustrated

INTRODUCTION

The game was $10-$20. I was in the big blind and Howard, sitting in seat 3, had posted an over-blind (i.e. a live straddle), thus making it $40 to go. He was becoming frustrated and said, 'Let's kick this game up.' Two players called after Howard, and the small blind made his bet up to $40. The pot was $180 and it was $20 to call. I held A♠-A♣ with only Howard left to act.

THE PLAY

Question 1: Should I: (a) pass (b) call (c) raise $50 (d) raise $200?

(a) ☐ (b) ☐ (c) ☐ (d) ☐ Points: ....

Action: I called and Howard checked. Curses, foiled again!

Flop: J♥-9♣-3♥. I held A♥-A♣ with $200 in the pot. Seat 1 checked, so the action was now on me, with three people still to act on this round.

Question 2: Should I: (a) check (b) bet $50 (c) bet $200?

(a) ☐ (b) ☐ (c) ☐ Points: ....

Action: I checked, intending to raise if there was action from just one opponent. Add five points if this was your plan. However, deduct two points if you intended just to call a bet from one of the players. Wake up! Everyone else checked.

Turn: J♥-9♣-3♥-3♦. I held A♥-A♣. The pot was still $200. Seat 1 checked.

Question 3: Should I: (a) check (b) bet $50 (c) bet $200?

(a) ☐ (b) ☐ (c) ☐ Points: ....

Action: I bet $200 and only Mike in the last seat called.

River: J♥-9♣-3♥-3♦-5♠. I held A♥-A♣ and the pot stood at $600.

Question 4: Should I: (a) check (b) bet $200 (c) bet $600?

(a) ☐ (b) ☐ (c) ☐ Points: ....

Total: ....

Action: I bet $500 and Mike called. I showed my aces and he showed his 7-7, saying gratuitously, 'I thought you were trying to steal the pot.'

Just a $1600 pot with a pair of aces. Oh well, had I raised, it might have been even less.

SCORECHART

40 This was the score I managed, with a bit of a struggle.

30-39 There are always different ways to play a hand. Danny and David both scored 36.

20-29 Mediocre.

10-19 You have some way to go before becoming a winning player.

0-9 Perhaps a different vocation, or take a vacation?

ANSWERS AND ANALYSIS

Holding: A♠-A♣.

Answer 1: (a) -5 (b) 10 (c) -2 (d) 6.

Howard usually raises when the action comes to him, while there may also be other players lurking in the deep grass. Why tip off my hand?

Flop: J♥-9♣-3♥.

Answer 2: (a) 5 (b) 0 (c) 10.

It is time to get this pot moving. I do not know where I am and, even if I am winning, it is very easy to be outdrawn with this kind of flop.

Turn: J♥-9♣-3♥-3♦.

Answer 3: (a) 1 (b) 0 (c) 10.

No-one has shown any interest in this pot so far. There is something to be said for getting it over with and getting on with the next hand. Somebody may think that I am trying to pinch the pot. Who, me? Perish the thought, would I do such a thing?

River: J♥-9♣-3♥-3♦-5♠.

Answer 4: (a) 0 (b) 2 (c) 10.

There is no reason to believe that I am losing. Perhaps I will get a call and perhaps not.

Hand 39

Hit me Baby!

INTRODUCTION

This hand was our standard £10-£20 blinds game. Bert had made it £80 to go in seat 4 and Cyril had called in seat 6. The pot stood at £190 and it was £80 to call. Jack held 5♥-5♦ in seat 8. He could see that there would be £2000 left to win from each of Bert and Cyril. A brief glance at the button and the two blinds had revealed nothing helpful.

THE PLAY

Question 1: Should Jack: (a) pass (b) call (c) raise £80 (d) raise £270?

(a) ☐	(b) ☐	(c) ☐	(d) ☐	Points: ....

Hypothetical Question 2: If there was £1000 left to win. Should Jack: (a) pass (b) call (c) raise £80 (d) raise £270?

(a) ☐	(b) ☐	(c) ☐	(d) ☐	Points: ....

Hypothetical Situation: Jack is in the big blind and everyone passes after Cyril, including the small blind. The pot is £190 and it is £60 to Jack.

Question 3: Should Jack: (a) pass (b) call (c) raise £60 (d) raise £250?

(a) ☐	(b) ☐	(c) ☐	(d) ☐	Points: ....

Action: Jack called, after which the button and the two blinds all passed.

Flop: 10♠-9♦-5♥. Jack held 5♥-5♦ with £270 in the pot. Bert now bet £250 and Cyril passed. The pot stood at £520.

Question 4: Should Jack: (a) pass (b) call (c) raise £250 (d) raise £750?

(a) ☐	(b) ☐	(c) ☐	(d) ☐	Points: ....

Action: Jack called, preferring to slowplay the hand with position.

Turn: 10♠-9♦-5♥-4♠. Jack held 5♥-5♦ and the pot was £770. Bert now bet £700, bringing the pot up to £1470. There was just £1050 left to raise.

Question 5: Should Jack: (a) pass (b) call (c) raise £750 (d) raise £1050 all-in?

(a) ☐	(b) ☐	(c) ☐	(d) ☐	Points: ....
				Total: ....

Action: Jack raised all-in and Bert passed. Jack won £1140 for his £80 stake. A 14/1 return is not at all bad for a 7/1 shot.

Hypothetical Action: Bert calls £1050 all-in and it turns out he held 10♥-10♣, which then stands up. Jack has now had a very bad day at the office so far. He has lost £2080 in the hand without ever having a real chance.

Reverse implied odds are often disregarded by poker players. It is true that they are less important in hold'em than in Omaha, a game in which the likelihood of two players holding good hands is much greater.

SCORECHART

50 Excellent.

40-49 Jack scored 48, while Danny and David scored 40.

25-39 Still in the acceptable range.

10-24 Where did you go wrong? This is such a standard coup.

0-9 If you scored -25, it is some type of record.

ANSWERS AND ANALYSIS

Holding: 5♥-5♦.

Answer 1: (a) 10 b) 8 (c) -5 (d) -2.

Jack is only getting £190/£80 odds. He may have the best hand, but this is irrelevant. If he misses the flop and Bert bets, he will have to pass anyway. Thus Jack is paying to hit the flop. It is about 7/1 against making a set. Jack can only justify calling on the basis of the implied odds of what he might make if things come good.

In the early stages of a tournament you would be even more likely to pass, in accordance with the law of conservation of chips.

Answer 2: (a) 10 (b) 0 (c) -5 (d) -5.

Jack's implied odds are now clearly inadequate.

Answer 3: (a) 10 (b) 2 (c) -5 (d) -5.

Although Jack has better odds in this situation, his position is compromised, since he will have to act first on every street.

Flop: 10♠-9♦-5♥.

Answer 4: (a) -5 (b) 10 (c) 0 (d) 6.

Jack has bought a ticket to the river. His only concern is how to get all the money into the pot. If he is already losing, well it will be back to the drawing board.

Turn: 10♠-9♦-5♥-4♠.

Answer 5: (a) -5 (c) 6 (c) 0 (d) 10.

With the prevailing chip situation, it is time to move in. Jack would have sulked for weeks if he just called, and Bert had A♠-9♠ and then made a backdoor flush for a monstrous outdraw.

Hand 40

Déjà vu

INTRODUCTION

Some months later, the same group of players were involved in another game with £10-£20 blinds. Bert had made it £80 to go in seat 5, and Alf had called in seat 6. Jack held J♣-10♣ in seat 7. The pot was £190 and it was £80 to call, with over £6000 left to bet.

THE PLAY

Question 1: Should Jack: (a) pass (b) call (c) raise £80 (d) raise £270?

(a) ☐	(b) ☐	(c) ☐	(d) ☐	Points: ....

Action: Jack called. Everyone passed to the small blind Ollie, who made a gay raise of £80. The big blind folded, and Bert and Alf both called. The pot stood at £580 and it was £80 to call.

Question 2: Should Jack: (a) pass (b) call (c) raise £80 (d) raise £660?

(a) ☐	(b) ☐	(c) ☐	(d) ☐	Points: ....

Flop: 9♣-8♦-4♥. Jack held J♣-10♣. Ollie checked, Bert bet £500 and Alf called, so the pot was now up to £1660.

Question 3: Should Jack: (a) pass (b) call (c) raise £500 (d) raise £2100?

(a) ☐	(b) ☐	(c) ☐	(d) ☐	Points: ....

Action: Jack called and Ollie passed.

Turn: 9♣-8♦-4♥-3♣. Jack held J♣-10♣. Bert now bet £1500 and Alf passed, so the pot was up to £3660. Jack would have £4000 left to bet if he were to call.

Question 4: Should Jack: (a) pass (b) call (c) raise £1500 (d) raise £4000 all-in?

(a) ☐	(b) ☐	(c) ☐	(d) ☐	Points: ....
				Total: ....

Action: Jack raised £4000 all-in. He remembered their previous encounter a few months before, when Bert had passed. Why not try the same thing this time? After all, it looks like almost an identical situation. Also, if the worst came to the worst, he could always improve. Thus there were two ways of winning the hand – Bert may pass again or Jack may make his draw. Even so, it is a mistake to raise. If Jack just calls here, all the energy lies with him. If he hits his hand, he has position on Bert and may well be called on the river.

This time Bert called.

River: 9♣-8♦-4♥-3♣-A♥. Jack held J♣-10♣. Bert held 9♥-8♥.

Thus on this occasion Bert won a satisfyingly (for him) big pot. Bert had made a little joke before the flop, raising with small suited connectors. Jack's pre-flop holding was much stronger than Bert's, yet the latter got the lolly. Ollie's baby raise simply kept the pot boiling. Had he made a man-sized raise, there is no doubt that both Bert and Jack would have thrown away their mediocre hands.

You are always more likely to be called when you are bluffing, than when you are betting with a good hand. There are two good reasons for this: sometimes people will read you correctly, and sometimes you may be representing the hand that your opponent actually holds, as happened here.

SCORECHART

40 You are more patient than I am.

30-39 Certainly if you called initially, then it is logical to call on the flop. I scored 36, Danny and David 32.

20-29 Jack only managed 26.

10-19 Extremely mediocre.

0-9 Awful. You cannot raise with just anything.

ANSWERS AND ANALYSIS

Holding: J♣-10♣.

Answer 1: (a) 10 (b) 6 (c) -5 (d) -5.

This is quite a good drawing hand. J-10 does not count as small connectors, since any straight draw you make will be to the nuts. That is the key difference from between this hand and 10♣-9♣; if it then comes K-Q, then a jack does not give you the nuts. With a drawing hand, however, the last thing you want to do is escalate the pot. It is marginal to call because there are still four players who may reraise. Well, we all like to live dangerously from time to time!

In the early stages of a tournament, this hand should be dumped, since it is too difficult to hit your hand. The law of conservation of chips rules, OK?

Answer 2: (a) 0 (b) 10 (c) -5 (d) -5.

This is a bit of a non-brainer. Jack would call blind with these odds. Quite what Ollie was playing at is unclear. Still, it is annoying that Jack has already had to wager £160 with such a mediocre hand.

Flop: 9♣-8♦-4♥.

Answer 3: (a) 10 (b) 6 (c) -5 (d) 2.

It is about 2/1 against making the straight by the river, but it is likely that there will be another full pot bet on the turn. Of course, if you hit a jack or ten, that may win. The pot odds are just not there, but what about the implied odds? If you hit the straight on the turn, you should be able to make some money. Could Alf have the same hand? It is unlikely.

Why not raise and try to take the pot away from your opponents? This would be a very dangerous ploy, but I commend your courage if you would do this in real life. If you want to draw to your hand, why not encourage Ollie to call as well?

Turn: 9♣-8♦-4♥-3♣.

Answer 4: (a) 0 (b) 10 (c) -5 (d) 4.

Jack now has a premium drawing hand and may have as many as 15 outs (nine clubs, three queens and three eights), assuming that a jack or ten will not be enough. He is about 2/1 against improving to a flush or a straight.

Hand 41

Beware

INTRODUCTION

I played this hand in my last no-limit tournament in Las Vegas. It has been adjusted to the pot-limit format, since there would have been very little difference in the play. You get to take over the mantle of my opponent, and thus have the privilege of playing against me.

It was part way through the first day, with many tables still in action, and the notional blinds were $100-$200. You held the second largest number of chips at the table, but I held a few more. Exactly how many, you did not know. You were in the big blind. Everyone had passed to Stewart, who raised the maximum $400 on the small blind. You hold K♠-9♠. There was $800 in the pot.

THE PLAY

Question 1: Should you: (a) pass (b) call (c) raise $400 (d) raise $1200?

(a) ☐	(b) ☐	(c) ☐	(d) ☐	Points: ....

Action: You called.

Flop: 9♣-5♠-2♥. You hold K♠-9♠ with $1200 in the pot. You have $15,600 in chips and Stewart has you covered. Stewart checked.

Question 2: Should you: (a) check (b) bet $500 (c) bet $1200?

(a) ☐	(b) ☐	(c) ☐	Points: ....

Action: You bet $1200.

Hypothetical Action: Stewart raises $3600, bringing the pot up to $7200.

Question 3: Should you: (a) pass (b) call (c) raise $4000 (d) raise $10,000?

(a) ☐	(b) ☐	(c) ☐	(d) ☐	Points: ....

Now back to the actual hand.

Action: Stewart flat called.

Hypothetical Turn: 9♣-5♠-2♥-7♣. You hold K♠-9♠. The pot stands at $3600 and you have $14,400 chips left. Stewart checks.

Question 4: Should you: (a) check (b) bet $1000 (c) bet $3600?

(a) ☐	(b) ☐	(c) ☐	Points: ....

Let us return to the real action.

Turn: 9♣-5♠-2♥-7♠. You hold K♠-9♠. There is $3600 in the pot and you have $14,400 in chips.

Hypothetical Action: Stewart bets $3600.

Question 5: Should you: (a) pass (b) call (c) raise $3600 (d) raise $10,800 all-in?

(a) ☐	(b) ☐	(c) ☐	(d) ☐	Points: ....

Action: In reality, Stewart checked.

Question 6: Should you: (a) check (b) bet $1000 (c) bet $3500?

(a) ☐	(b) ☐	(c) ☐	Points: ....

Action: You bet $3600. Well, remember, the real player who I faced in this hand did not know me at all. He fell headlong into the trap. Stewart raised the entire pot, $10,800 all-in.

If you realised, from the number of chips I stipulated, that this was what was going to happen, then score two extra points. I'll bluff you on another occasion.

Question 7: Should you: (a) pass (b) call all-in?

(a) ☐	(b) ☐	Points: ....
		Total: ....

Action: You called. Well, let's drop that pretence. He called. I hope you would never have got in the situation and then, if you did, would have had the sense to pass here.

River: 9♣-5♠-2♥-7♠-J♠. You hold K♠-9♠. Stewart held 9♠-9♦.

Thus my opponent doubled his money and I was left with just a few chips. In actual fact he only had eight outs, since I had the other two nines, the three kings were no use to him, and the 2♠ would have made me a full house. Moreover, in reality this was no-limit and I set him in for more than the pot, so he did not even receive 2/1 for his chips.

For the next three hours of the tournament I kept on going all-in with just an ace. My hand would stand up, but then my meagre store would dwindle down again. Eventually I went bust on a different table; I don't know how my brave challenger fared.

SCORECHART

72 A mirror image of my play. David also scored 70. We do not want you in our game.

60-70 You are both patient and aggressive in the right situations.

45-59 My real-life opponent fell in love with his hand. Did you fall into the same trap? He scored 40/60. We do not know his answer to the hypothetical question. Danny scored 50.

30-44 I hope that this was not your finest hour.

15-29 A truly unsatisfactory performance.

0-14 Unbelievably bad.

ANSWERS AND ANALYSIS

Holding: K♠-9♠.

Answer 1: (a) 0 (b) 10 (c) 1 (d) 2.

This is a fairly good hand. Gap theory suggests that I would have bet with a hand in the top 50% of all hands, so you should call with one in the top 33%, and raise with one in the top 16%. For example, 9-8 would be good enough for a call, whereas one would want Q-J or a pair of eights at the minimum for a reraise.

Flop: 9♣-5♠-2♥.

Answer 2: (a) 2 (b) 4 (c) 10.

Top pair, good kicker is a very good hand when there are only two players in the pot, but it is not so strong that it should be slowplayed.

Answer 3: (a) 10 (b) 3 (c) 2 (d) 0.

Stewart's check was suspicious. It is normal practice is to bet with only one opponent after you have raised pre-flop. A check-raise suggests that he holds big pair such as aces or kings. It would be easy to lose big in this pot, so it is better to pass. Occasionally you will have been bluffed out, but there is no shame in passing.

Answer 4: (a) 10 (b) 2 (c) 6.

This is still a pretty good hand. Stewart may hold A♣-Q♣, so why give him a free card? On the other hand, a softly, softly approach is better here.

Turn: 9♣-5♠-2♥-7♠.

Answer 5: (a) 0 (b) 10 (c) 0 (d) 3.

You have a good hand, but why has Stewart bet? Conceivably he holds a better flush draw than you with A♠-Q♠, but then you would still be favourite, since he only has 13 outs. Alternatively, he might have a big pair and therefore does not want to allow a free card. Admittedly $3600 is quite a high proportion of your chips. You do not know exactly what is going on, but you do have a good hand.

Answer 6: (a) 10 (b) 3 (c) 0.

Your draw is too big for you to consider betting. Stewart has played this hand in a mysterious fashion. Had he bet, passed or even raised on the flop, that would have all been normal. But his passive play is most odd. Surely he has a very big pair in the hole? A small bet may be okay, since you do have a very strong hand. However, this play would make more sense if you were still able to make a pot-sized bet on the river, even if you are forced to call a raise from Stewart here.

Even if you are not winning with your top pair right now, all the energy lies with you on the river. You may hit a spade, a nine or a king and get paid off. Anyway, why do you feel the need to bet? If you are winning, it is very hard for you to be outdrawn. If you are losing and connect on the river, then you may get paid off at no risk whatsoever.

This is an example of 'Morton's fork', which was explained earlier in the book. You gain if you check and are winning, but you also gain if you are losing.

Answer 7: (a) 10 (b) 0.

This simply becomes an exercise in arithmetic. Imagine that Stewart holds A♥-A♦, which is about the best scenario you can hope for. You have now 'seen' the four cards of the turn, your two cards and Stewart's two cards, leaving 44 unknown. You will win with nine spades, two nines and three kings, 14 cards. You are getting precisely 2/1 for your money and 14 wins out of 44 cards is worse than 2/1 against. There are no implied odds, because it is all-in, so it is a clear pass. In fact, it is even worse than that. This is a tournament, so if you do not improve, you are out of the competition.

You do not have to figure this out ever again. If you think that you have 14 outs or less at hold'em, with one card to come, then you have inadequate odds for an all-in pot call. Make it 15, and you're fine.

Hand 42

The Importance of the Kicker

INTRODUCTION

This hand was played with blinds of £10-£20. Ray, a very loose player with a mountain of chips, was first to act after the blinds, holding A♣-8♣.

THE PLAY

Question 1: Should he: (a) pass (b) call (c) raise £20 (d) raise £60?

(a) ☐	(b) ☐	(c) ☐	(d) ☐	Points: ....

Action: Ray called and Bill, in seat 4, immediately raised £80. Craig, Ed and Fred all called and both blinds passed. There was now £450 in the pot and it was £80 to Ray.

Question 2: Should he: (a) pass (b) call (c) raise £80 (d) raise £530?

(a) ☐	(b) ☐	(c) ☐	(d) ☐	Points: ....

Flop: K♣-Q♦-7♣. Ray held A♣-8♣. The pot was £530.

Question 3: Should you: (a) check (b) bet £100 (c) bet £530?

(a) ☐	(b) ☐	(c) ☐	Points: ....

Action: Ray bet £100. Bill raised £600 and both Craig and Fred called, while Ed passed. Now it was £600 to Ray with £2730 in the pot and bundles still left to bet.

Question 4: Should you: (a) pass (b) call (c) raise £500 (d) raise £3300?

(a) ☐	(b) ☐	(c) ☐	(d) ☐	Points: ....

Action: Ray called.

Turn: K♣-Q♦-7♣-9♥. Ray held A♣-8♣ and there was £3330 in the pot.

Question 5: Should Ray: (a) check (b) bet £500 (c) bet £3330?

(a) ☐	(b) ☐	(c) ☐	Points: ....

Action: Ray and Bill both checked, Craig bet £3300 and Fred called. There was £9,930 in the pot and it was £3300 to Ray. If he called there would be £5700 left to bet.

Question 6: Should you: (a) pass (b) call (c) raise £5700 all-in?

(a) ☐	(b) ☐	(c) ☐	Points: ....

Action: Ray called and Bill raised £5700 all-in. That is the last thing that Ray wanted. Both Craig and Fred called, so the pot now stood at £33,630.

Question 7: Should you: (a) pass (b) call all-in?

(a) ☐	(b) ☐	Points: ....
		Total: ....

River: K♣-Q♦-7♣-9♥-6♦. Ray held A♣-8♣. Both Craig and Fred had J-10 and split the pot. In fact Fred had J♠-10♠ and Craig held J♣-10♣. What a hand Craig had! Poor Bill had Q♠-Q♦.

Thus Ray contrived to lose nearly £10,000 in the one hand. He too was poorer, but we should not waste any sympathy on him. He made three errors in this pot: calling the first bet; betting £100 on the flop, which made the pot unnecessarily big; and making the first call on the turn.

I have a confession to make. I invented this hand as a cautionary tale. It illustrates several important points. First, if you start off with mediocre hands, then it is an uphill battle. (A nut flush draw with a kicker higher than the 8♣ would have offered Ray better prospects of winning the pot. The 9♣ might have provided an extra out on the turn, the 10♣ or J♣ would have given him gutshot straight outs, and the Q♣ would have made him a pair on the flop, to go with his draw.) Second, you must obey the odds, not the dictates of your heart. Third, small bets can cause a pot to escalate hugely. And finally, you should not fall in love with nut flush draws.

SCORECHART

70 Well done. But I might have called that first £20 and only scored 65.

60-69 That's fine. David scored 65.

45-59 The mythical Ray scored 48. Look where that got him. Danny scored 52.

30-44 I hope you would have lost less money than Ray, at any rate.

15-29 If this is typical of your scores, then I admire your perseverance.

0-14 Ouch!

ANSWERS AND ANALYSIS

Holding: A♣-8♣.

Answer 1: (a) 10 (b) 5 (c) 2 (d) 3.

This is a perfectly satisfactory call, or even raise, for Ray. That is the way, win or lose, he wants to play poker. I hope you have higher aspirations. Out of position, as here, this should normally be passed.

Answer 2: (a) 0 (b) 10 (c) 0 (d) 0.

Regardless of whether you have Ray's profile, you now have both the pot odds and implied odds for this call. This has become like a limit raise hand. You notice the way in which a player like Ray galvanises the game.

Flop: K♣-Q♦-7♣.

Answer 3: (a) 10 (b) 1 (c) 0.

Ray has a good hand, but with two picture cards out and four opponents, it is certain that at least one player has hit his flop. The circumspect move is to check and await developments.

Answer 4: (a) -5 (b) 10 (c) -5 (d) 0.

Ray is getting 9/2 for his money. His odds against improving on the next card are 38/9, only slightly worse than 4/1, and there also are the implied odds if he improves. It would be a dreadful mistake to pass. I do have considerable sympathy with the idea of going all-in here. If you get even two callers, then you will have ample pot odds. However, the fact that everyone was playing with lots of money means that it was physically impossible to make an all-in raise in this case. In fact, there was £9000 left to bet if Ray were to call.

Turn: K♣-Q♦-7♣-9♥.

Answer 5: (a) 10 (b) -2 (c) -5.

Ray has a good drawing hand, but it is just that.

Answer 6: (a) 10 (b) 2 (c) -5.

It is still about 4/1 against making a flush. You are only getting just over 3/1 for your money, so it is correct to pass. You cannot, with confidence, say that your implied odds are 4/1 because Bill will probably call after you. Also, you cannot be certain anybody will call your flush if you make it on the river. And of course, you cannot be sure that either the Q♣ or 9♣ will not give one of your opponents a full house. It would be barmy to raise here. If you do call, you want Bill to do so as well.

Answer 7: (a) -5 (b) 10.

You have 6/1 for your money about a 4/1 shot. You must now call. To pass would be a crime against nature.

Hand 43

Getting there

INTRODUCTION

This hand occurred in a £5-£10 game. It matters very little how big the game is, since the same principles apply whatever the size. It is the way the players vary that counts.

Al in seat 3 had made it £30 to go. Fred had called, as had Joe and Tim. The pot stood at £135 and it was £30 to call. Ray, whom we met for the first time in the previous hand, held K♠-J♦ in seat 8. Fiery, whom I first ran into under various pseudonyms about 50 years ago, was on the button in seat 9.

THE PLAY

Question 1: Did *Ray*: (a) pass (b) call (c) raise £30 (d) raise £165?

(a) ☐	(b) ☐	(c) ☐	(d) ☐	Points: ....

Question 2: Would *you*: (a) pass (b) call (c) raise £30 (d) raise £165?

(a) ☐	(b) ☐	(c) ☐	(d) ☐	Points: ....

Action: Ray called. Fiery, in seat 9, raised £195. The blinds both folded and Al and Fred called. Joe then folded, but Tim also called. The pot stood at £975 and it was £195 to Ray. Fred had approximately £3000 remaining and Tim only had £2000 left. Al, Fiery and Ray each had well over £10,000.

Question 3: Did *Ray*: (a) pass (b) call (c) raise £195 (d) raise £1170?

(a) ☐	(b) ☐	(c) ☐	(d) ☐	Points: ....

Question 4: Should *you*: (a) pass (b) call (c) raise £195 (d) raise £1170?

(a) ☐	(b) ☐	(c) ☐	(d) ☐	Points: ....

Action: Ray called, bringing the pot up to £1170. Once again, the action has been galvanised.

Flop: Q♥-10♦-7♠. Ray held K♠-J♦. Al bet £800 and Fred and Tim both called. The pot now stood at £3570.

Question 5: Did *Ray*: (a) pass (b) call (c) raise £800 (d) raise £4500?

(a) ☐	(b) ☐	(c) ☐	(d) ☐	Points: ....

Question 6: Should *you*: (a) pass (b) call (c) raise £800 (d) raise £4400?

(a) ☐	(b) ☐	(c) ☐	(d) ☐	Points: ....

Action: Ray called, as did Fiery. Well, that's a relief. The pot was now £5170.

Turn: Q♥-10♦-7♠-9♣. Ray held K♠-J♦. Al checked, Fred bet £2000 all-in and Tim called all-in for £1000. The main pot stood at £7170 with a further £1000 in the side pot. Ray had £12,000 left on the table, as did Al and Fiery.

Question 7: Did *Ray*: (a) pass (b) call (c) raise £2000 (d) raise £4000 (e) raise £10,000 all-in?

(a) ☐	(b) ☐	(c) ☐	(d) ☐	(e) ☐	Points: ....

Question 8: Should *you*: (a) pass (b) call (c) raise £2000 (d) raise £4000 (e) raise £10,000 all-in?

(a) ☐	(b) ☐	(c) ☐	(d) ☐	(e) ☐	Points: ....

Action: Ray called, Fiery pondered and called, but Al passed.

River: Q♥-10♦-7♠-9♣-5♠. Ray held K♠-J♦. The main pot stood at £9170 and the side pot at £3000. The dealer reminded the table that there was still further betting.

Question 9: Should either Ray or you: (a) check (b) bet £2000 (c) bet £10,000 all-in?

(a) ☐	(b) ☐	(c) ☐	Points: ....

Action: Ray bet £3000. Fiery immediately passed, showing his A♣-K♣ in the process and saying, 'You were taking a big risk there.' Ray showed the nuts and the other players threw in their hands. Fiery muttered and said that he would have passed, if Ray had been a man and raised on the turn.

Question 10: Was Fiery getting adequate odds to justify his call: (a) no (b) possibly (c) yes?

(a) ☐	(b) ☐	(c) ☐	Points: ....
			Total: ....

SCORECHART

100 It is interesting trying to work out what other people would do. Poker is very much about empathy. David scored 91.

90-99 An excellent score.

75-89 Satisfactory. Danny scored 84 and Ray scored 46/60.

60-74 You may have become confused by the unusual format of this hand.

40-59 This is rather dispiriting.

20-39 I hope that you did not pass when you had pot odds.

0-19 Making a negative score would surely be some kind of record.

ANSWERS AND ANALYSIS

Holding: K♠-J♦.

Answer 1: (a) 0 (b) 10 (c) 2 (d) -3.

Ray does not play in the game to pass.

Answer 2: (a) 10 (b) 5 (c) -1 (d) -5.

This hand ranks a fairly long way from the top in the pre-flop rankings. So many people have already called that it is quite likely some of the cards that you are looking for are in their hands. Having said that, there are only three people left who may raise. You have excellent position and might die of boredom waiting for a better spot. But wait a moment. What about Fiery? He has still to act. What was a fairly reasonable call becomes a definite pass. With a player like Ray still to act you would be more inclined to call, but someone like Fiery should frighten you off.

Answer 3: (a) 0 (b) 10 (c) -1 (d) -5.

Ray is not the last of the big passers. It did not seem to bother him that he had been whip-lashed.

Answer 4: (a) 10 (b) 4 (c) -5 (d) -3.

Clearly you do not have the best hand, and some players probably have better drawing hands than you. You would be better off with small suited connectors in a situation like this. In order to hit your flop, you need something of a miracle. The reward/risk ratio is basically the same as the first time round, but the reward relative to the cost is much smaller. At first potentially you might have won £5000 for £30. Now it is the same sum for £195. Another disturbing feature is the fact that the last raiser is looking over your shoulder. Your position is not as good as you might have hoped.

Flop: Q♥-10♦-7♠.

Answer 5: (a) -5 (b) 10 (c) -5 (d) 5.

Answer 6: (a) 3 (b) 10 (c) -5 (d) -5.

The fact that Ray is a loose player does not enter into it. You have slightly better than 11/2 for your money and it is less than 5/1 against completing the straight on the next card. There is also the matter of implied odds. People may not believe you have made the nuts. Sometimes they may become confused and think that a nine would only make an inside straight, whereas here K-J is the most logical draw.

However, there are some concerns. Someone may have the same hand, although this seems unlikely. Also you may not have the full eight outs – surely at least one ace has gone, with so many people in the pot. Finally, Fiery may raise and others may pass, causing your pot odds to diminish sharply.

Turn: Q♥-10♦-7♠-9♣.

Answer 7: (a) -5 (b) 10 (c) 0 (d) 1 (e) 10.

Answer 8: (a) -5 (b) 7 (c) 0 (d) 10 (e) 1.

Ray is more likely to call, in order to keep people in. Also, his image is such that Al and Fiery may not have realised he has hit the nuts. Calling is a dangerous strategy, since if an open pair comes, then it will be difficult to pass on the river. But it does set a trap. Al or, more likely, Fiery may take it in to their heads to raise. You can be patient here, since the money can be bet on the river.

If you believe that either of the players still to act has trips, then you should raise. But it does not need be all the money. A £4000 raise would be very tempting, and neither player would have the correct odds to call. It will cost either player £6000 to win £14,000. The odds of filling up with a set are around 7/2, and it is very likely that some of your opponents have cards that already pair with the board, thus reducing their number of outs. If Ray were to raise, then he would be more likely to raise the maximum. Since he himself would call an all-in raise with trips, he would expect his opponents to do the same. The problem is, if you do raise, you cannot really be bluffing at this stage. Two players are already all-in, so why would you reraise except with a very strong hand? Thus you are less likely to be able to attract anyone to call your raise.

River: Q♥-10♦-7♠-9♣-5♠.

Answer 9: (a) 0 (b) 10 (c) 4.

There is no point in checking, since Fiery is clearly not going to bet. A smallish bet has a better chance of securing a call. Ray is an experienced player, so it is unlikely that he will play any differently from you or I in this situation.

Answer 10: (a) 10 (b) 2 (c) 0.

Fiery is risking £2000 to win £10,170. This is only 5/1, and from his viewpoint he is 21/2 against hitting a jack to make the nuts, which is just hopeless odds. But what about his implied odds? Al may call, giving him 6/1 on the turn, but he may also raise. What about Fiery's chance of getting called if a jack comes on the river? That seems unlikely. He would be betting into a virtually dead side pot and thus could not be bluffing. Thus it was correct for Fiery to pass. In the actual pot, any of us would have called here with the second straight, but then Fiery would have had to admit that he was 14/1 against making the middle-pin straight.

Hand 44

Empathy

INTRODUCTION

In this £10-£20 blinds game, Alan and Bob were the only callers in seats 5 and 7. Art held Q♥-J♥ in seat 8. There was £70 in the pot and it was £20 to him.

THE PLAY

Question 1: Should he: (a) pass (b) call (c) raise £20 (d) raise £100?

(a) ☐ (b) ☐ (c) ☐ (d) ☐ Points: ....

Action: Art made it £120. The button passed, as did both blinds, but Alan and Bob both called.

Flop: J♣-8♦-3♣. Art held Q♥-J♥. Alan now bet £390 and Bob passed. There was £780 in the pot and £6000 left to bet.

Question 2: Should Art: (a) pass (b) call (c) raise £700 (d) raise £1170?

(a) ☐ (b) ☐ (c) ☐ (d) ☐ Points: ....

Action: Art raised £800 and Alan called.

Turn: J♣-8♦-3♣-A♦. Art held Q♥-J♥. The pot now stood at £2770 and Alan had £5200 left to bet. He checked.

Question 3: Should Art: (a) check (b) bet £500 (c) bet £1000 (d) bet £2700?

(a) ☐ (b) ☐ (c) ☐ (d) ☐ Points: ....

Action: Art checked.

River: J♣-8♦-3♣-A♦-5♥. Art held Q♥-J♥. Alan now bet £2500, bringing the pot up to £5270.

Question 4: Should Art: (a) pass (b) call (c) raise £2700 all-in.

(a) ☐ (b) ☐ (c) ☐ Points: ....

Total: ....

Action: Art called. Alan held K♦-J♦ and won a nice pot. As he raked in the chips, he said: 'I would have passed, had you bet the turn.' People often say this type of thing, sometimes with the intent of needling the opposition. However, on this occasion it may well have been true. Like Art, Alan was worried that his opponent may have been holding A♣-X♣. Two minds with but a single thought! Aggression so often pays off in poker, since it gives you another way of winning the pot.

What if Art had raised on the river? Well, this must be a better play than flat calling. I think that in Alan's shoes, I would have had the pot stolen from underneath my nose in this particular scenario.

SCORECHART

40 My score, but it is just a matter of opinion.

30-39 It may be more profitable to play this way.

20-29 You may have played too defensively. David scored 29 and Danny could only manage 22.

10-19 Well, at least other players like to see you at the table.

4-9 That is just amazingly bad.

ANSWERS AND ANALYSIS

Holding: Q♥-J♥.

Answer 1: (a) -1 (b) 4 (c) 3 (d) 10.

This is a pretty decent hand in good position. It is worth a raise here to get rid of the tourists. If the players who have already limped in then reraise, then you'll know that they are very strong and can act accordingly, which should usually mean you will pass. Of course, you are risking being raised out with a hand that has reasonable potential.

Flop: J♣-8♦-3♣.

Answer 2: (a) 0 (b) 7 (c) 2 (d) 10.

Normally players check to the original raiser if they have a big made hand, so Alan could be on a draw. If Art just calls here, and then calls again on both the turn and river, then he may go off in a big way. Alan is too good a player not to bet out occasionally with A-J or even low trips. You could consider making an in-between raise. Then, if Alan reraises, you can reassess the situation. Of course you must not make this play too often with the same kind of hand or your strategy will become transparent.

Turn: J♣-8♦-3♣-A♦.

Answer 3: (a) 10 (b) 1 (c) 5 (d) 3.

Whenever an ace comes with a two flush on the table, it is possible that your opponent has made a pair of aces, while drawing to the nut flush. In our example, it is very likely that he could have A♣-X♣. Even if you bet, you still won't know whether you are coming or going, since Alan could flat call with A♣-8♣. Thus a check is more circumspect.

River: J♣-8♦-3♣-A♦-5♥.

Answer 4: (a) 10 (b) 4 (c) 8.

Art's check on the turn may have served to induce a river bet from his opponent. Or Alan may actually have the better hand. This is always the problem when you go into passive mode.

Hand 45

Aiming for the Scoop

INTRODUCTION

Again this hand took place in a £10-£20 blinds game. Ian was in seat 5 and had made it £80 to go, and Ralph had called in seat 6. Tim held K♦-Q♦ on the button. There is £190 in the pot.

THE PLAY

Question 1: Should Tim: (a) pass (b) call (c) raise £80 (d) raise £270?

(a) ☐	(b) ☐	(c) ☐	(d) ☐	Points: ....

Action: Tim raised £270.

Hypothetical Action: Everyone passes to Ralph, who had just called in the first instance. He now raises £800. The pot is £1610 and it is £800 to play.

Question 2: Should Tim: (a) pass (b) call (c) raise £800 (d) raise £2400 all-in?

(a) ☐	(b) ☐	(c) ☐	(d) ☐	Points: ....

Returning to the real hand.

Action: Tim raised £270 and both Ian and Ralph called.

Flop: A♠-J♥-10♦. Tim holds K♦-Q♦. The pot stands at £1080 and everyone has large sums left to bet. Ian and Ralph both check.

Question 3: Should Tim: (a) check (b) bet £200 (c) bet £600 (d) bet £1080?

(a) ☐	(b) ☐	(c) ☐	(d) ☐	Points: ....

Action: Tim bet £1000, Ian called and Ralph raised £3000. The pot is £7080 and it is £3000 to Tim. There is £30,000 left to bet against both players.

Question 4: Should Tim: (a) pass (b) call (c) raise £3000 (d) raise £13,000?

(a) ☐	(b) ☐	(c) ☐	(d) ☐	Points: ....

Action: Tim called and Ian passed.

Turn: A♠-J♥-10♦-7♣. Tim held K♦-Q♦. Ralph bet £7000. The pot was £17,080, and if Tim called, there was still £23,000 left to bet.

Question 5: Should Tim: (a) pass (b) call (c) raise £23,000 all-in?

(a) ☐	(b) ☐	(c) ☐	Points: ....

Action: Tim called.

River: A♠-J♥-10♦-7♣-A♥. Tim held K♦-Q♦ and there was £24,080 in the pot. Ralph checked.

Question 6: Should Tim: (a) check (b) bet £8000 (c) bet £23,000 all-in?

(a) ☐	(b) ☐	(c) ☐	Points: ....
			Total: ....

Action: Tim bet £23,000 and Ralph called. Ralph's hand was J♠-J♦ and he won a £70,080 pot. Ralph now said: 'I was worried that you had trip aces, but that was unlikely once the ace came on the river.'

That remains the biggest loss of Tim's career, and he still has nightmares about the hand. That being so, he probably should have raised all-in on the turn. For most sports, the pain of losing is greater than the joy of winning. But the aphorism, no pain no gain, has no meaning in poker.

Would Ralph have passed facing a raise from Tim on the turn? We will never know, though clearly he should do so. Have you noticed that he always bet less than the pot? Did he know what he was doing, or was he just lucky? Why did he play strongly on the earlier streets and then check when he made the winning full house? That remains a mystery.

What is not a mystery is that Tim is still around, alive and kicking – and sometimes screaming, whereas Ralph has vanished from the scene.

SCORECHART

60 My own score. Tim made 58. playing perfect poker. David would also have lost his money; he managed 54.

50-59 Excellent. Presumably you would have lost less money.

40-49 Still satisfactory.

25-39 Are you sure that you understand hold'em? Well, Danny only scored 32.

10-24 That's terrible.

0-9 Do not play with money you cannot afford to lose, except against me!

ANSWERS AND ANALYSIS

Holding: K♦-Q♦.

Answer 1: (a) -2 (b) 0 (c) 7 (d) 10.

This a pretty good hand, but activity has already taken place. Let us apply extended gap theory. Ian would raise with a hand in the top 50%, and Ralph should call with one in the top 33%. Tim should also call with one in the top 33%, but raise with one in the top 16%. K♦-Q♦ certainly fits the bill here, but there is a problem...

Answer 2: (a) 10 (b) 0 (c) -2 (d) -5.

Ralph slowplayed the hand at first and has now come on extremely aggressively. He probably has a pair of aces or kings, but even A-K has Tim heavily dominated. He must pass. That is not so important by itself. What matters is that, by playing aggressively, he has missed out on the strong drawing potential of his hand. Frankly, I wouldn't worry too much about this here, since if Ralph were to reraise here then Tim's hand was probably badly dominated anyhow. Ultimately, it is your decision. Are you happy to see a nice hand waste away? If so, then go ahead and make the second raise. If not, just call. Just remember, in the long run, aggression is more profitable in poker.

Flop: A♠-J♥-10♦.

Answer 3: (a) 4 (b) 4 (c) 10 (d) 8.

You do not make such a tremendous hand every day of the week. The trick now is to turn it into a good profit. You could choose to slowplay the hand by checking, which should generate a small profit. In some ways a smallish bet might be more suspicious than full-blooded pot bet. However, this flop may have hit either or both players, so the way to win big is to bet out. Of course, if you bet and everyone passes, you will be disappointed. Can you cope with this? There is no easy answer. It depends on your personality.

Answer 4: (a) -5 (b) 10 (c) 2 (d) 6.

You are in tremendously good shape here, since you can only be beaten if the board pairs, or by a backdoor flush. If both players are trying to make full houses, their hands interfere with one another. However, if one player has the made straight with you and the other has a set, then going all-in at this stage is not a bad outcome from his point of view. He will fill up around 35% of the time. Another consideration is the fact that you don't want Ian to pass. Thus it is better to let a card come off here.

Turn: A♠-J♥-10♦-7♣.

Answer 5: (a) -5 (b) 10 (c) 8.

Surely Ralph has the same straight as Tim? Neither can improve and the pot may as well be over. However, Ralph cannot be certain that Tim has the straight. A thoughtful call may provide a smoke screen. Then, if the board pairs on the river, Tim can try to bluff at it. After all, he has position on Ralph.

On the other hand, this is an enormous pot. Why not raise all-in? Then there can be no mistakes and no regrets. It depends how you want to play poker. What is your internal fortitude? There is nothing wrong with being a bit chicken and raising all-in. That may seem paradoxical. However, when you know you are winning, raising the maximum is the easiest way to play poker, though not necessarily the most profitable.

River: A♠-J♥-10♦-7♣-A♥.

Answer 6: (a) 6 (b) 0 (b) 10.

This is the situation that Tim was aiming for, so he should go to it! This is admirable play. If you decided to check now because the pot was too big for your nerves, then that's fair enough. I hope that in that case you raised all-in on the turn. If you did not do so, and now decided to check, then deduct two points. It is illogical to play this way.

Hand 46

Getting a move on

INTRODUCTION

The blinds were £5-£10. Alec had limped in immediately after the blinds, and Bert then made it £50 to play. Craig and Ollie both called, as did the small blind, Ron. Sid held 7♥-6♦ in the big blind. It was £40 to him with £220 in the pot.

THE PLAY

Question 1: Should Sid: (a) pass (b) call (c) raise £50 (d) raise £260?

(a) ☐	(b) ☐	(c) ☐	(d) ☐	Points: ....

Action: Sid called and Alec passed. I do not understand why, since he is getting 13/2 for his money here. He has just frittered away £10. This is one way that players lose tournaments. They squander small sums by limping in, thereby disobeying the law of conservation of chips. It is not quite such a cardinal sin in cash games, but it is still very bad.

Flop: Q♠-7♥-6♣. Sid held 7♥-6♦. The pot stood at £260. Ron, first to act, checked.

Question 2: Should Sid: (a) check (b) bet £50 (c) bet £250?

(a) ☐	(b) ☐	(c) ☐	Points: ....

Action: Sid bet £250, and both Bert and Ollie called.

Turn: Q♠-7♥-6♣-3♠. Sid held 7♥-6♦ with £1010 in the pot and £5000 left to bet.

Question 3: Should Sid: (a) check (b) bet £250 (c) bet £500 (d) bet £1000?

(a) ☐	(b) ☐	(c) ☐	(d) ☐	Points: ....

Action: Sid bet £900, Bert called and Ollie passed.

River: Q♠-7♥-6♣-3♠-8♠. Sid held 7♥-6♦. The pot was now up to £2810 and there was £4100 left to bet.

Question 4: Should Sid: (a) check (b) bet £1000 (c) bet £2000 (d) bet £2800?

(a) ☐	(b) ☐	(c) ☐	(d) ☐	Points: ....

Action: Sid bet £2000 and Bert raised £2100 all-in. The pot stood at £8910.

Question 5: Should Sid: (a) pass (b) call?

(a) ☐	(b) ☐	Points: ....
		Total: ....

Action: Sid called, Bert showed down A♠-Q♥ and Sid had doubled up. Bert then enlightened us, saying, 'I didn't believe you had a straight or flush.' Well, he was certainly correct in that one respect!

SCORECHART

50 Another day I would decide differently.

40-49 Probably just as good a score.

30-39 Even this is not too bad. David scored 34.

20-29 This is highly unsatisfactory. Danny made 29.

5-19 Simply atrocious.

ANSWERS AND ANALYSIS

Holding: 7♥-6♦.

Answer 1: (a) 2 (b) 10 (c) -2 (d) -5.

This is not much of a hand and Sid is in poor position, but he is getting 11/2 for his money and only Alec can reraise.

Flop: Q♠-7♥-6♣.

Answer 2: (a) 8 (b) 3 (c) 10.

All the answers here are reasonable alternatives. It used to be received wisdom that you should check a good hand to the original bettor, in order to reraise when he bets. The disadvantage of this approach is that it may well end the pot there and then. There is also the danger that it might just be checked around, and all your opponents have a free card with which to beat you. In the excellent *Super/System*, Doyle Brunson wrote that he would always bet out in this kind of situation. However, at that time, betting was his most common choice in any situation! It is also possible to make a gay bet, which will have the effect of leaving your opponents mystified. But, if you do bet the full amount, then that will also leave them puzzled. They may think that you have four to a straight. You are doomed against trips, but otherwise it is very unlikely that you could be behind here. Ultimately, this is the kind of situation where you should vary your play.

Turn: Q♠-7♥-6♣-3♠.

Answer 3: (a) 0 (b) 0 (c) 4 (d) 10.

It is inconceivable that either Bert or Ollie could be drawing dead here. It is even possible that Ollie has made the straight. But then, from their viewpoint, you may have made that same hand yourself. It is best to bet and review the situation if you are raised. If you check and Bert bets, you will have no means of knowing whether or not you are winning.

River: Q♠-7♥-6♣-3♠-8♠.

Answer 4: (a) 10 (b) 8 (c) 9 (d) 5.

It really depends on your perception of Bert, how you think he perceives you, and your overall attitude to risk management. Against an inveterate caller or a weak player, the situation is crying out for a bet. They will not be bluffing if they bet when you decide to check. But if you bet, surely you cannot be bluffing? Thus a good player will only call you if you are beaten. Against a seasoned campaigner like Bert, a check may therefore be in order.

Answer 5: (a) 2 (b) 10.

You must make a crying call, since Bert's play is just too puzzling. It is most unlikely that he has made a flush, since what would he have been calling you with on the flop? It would have to be A♠-K♠. In fact, it would have been far more worrying had the turn and river brought two hearts instead of two spades, i.e. Q♠-7♥-6♣-3♥-8♥. In that case the scenario of A♥-Q♥ is entirely feasible. I would definitely have checked that board on the river.

Hand 47

Hoist by your own Petard

INTRODUCTION

The blinds were £10-£20 in this hand. The players in seats 3, 4 and 5 had all passed. Tony held 9♥-9♣ in seat 6. The pot stood at £30. It was £20 to Tony.

THE PLAY

Question 1: Should Tony: (a) pass (b) call (c) raise £20 (d) raise £60?

(a) ☐	(b) ☐	(c) ☐	(d) ☐	Points: ....

Action: Tony raised £60 and only Boris in seat 7 called. So far, so good! Boris is a dangerous opponent. We give him a lot of respect but try not to make that also a lot of money.

Flop: J♥-7♠-3♦. Tony held 9♥-9♣. The pot stood at £190.

Question 2: Should Tony: (a) check (b) bet £20 (c) bet £100 (d) bet £190?

(a) ☐	(b) ☐	(c) ☐	(d) ☐	Points: ....

Action: Tony bet £150 and Boris called.

Turn: J♥-7♠-3♦-8♣. Tony held 9♥-9♣ with £490 in the pot.

Question 3: Should Tony: (a) check (b) bet £100 (c) bet £300 (d) bet £490?

(a) ☐	(b) ☐	(c) ☐	(d) ☐	Points: ....

Action: Tony checked and Boris bet £150. The pot stood at £640.

Question 4: Should Tony: (a) pass (b) call (c) raise £150 (d) raise £790?

(a) ☐	(b) ☐	(c) ☐	(d) ☐	Points: ....

Action: Tony called £150.

River: J♥-7♠-3♦-8♣-9♦. Tony held 9♥-9♣. The pot stood at £790.

Question 5: Should Tony: (a) check (b) bet £150 (c) bet £790?

(a) ☐	(b) ☐	(c) ☐	Points: ....

Action: Tony checked and Boris bet £790. The pot stood at £1580.

Question 6: Should Tony: (a) pass (b) call (c) raise £790 (d) raise £2370? If he does raise the full amount, then Boris will only have £500 further with which to reraise.

(a) ☐	(b) ☐	(c) ☐	(d) ☐	Points: ....
				Total: ....

Action: Tony called and Boris showed down J♠-10♠. Tony mucked his hand, saying disgustedly, 'A last card middle-pin.' Of course we now know why Boris did not bet out the full amount on the turn. He turned chicken and bet small, fearing being raised and possibly taken off his hand. His poor play netted him a nice pot.

'Why,' Tony thought ruefully, 'couldn't it have come a ten instead?'

Somebody whispered to Tony: 'What did you have?'

'Queens,' was the dishonest answer.

'Why not raise on the turn?'

Tony patiently explained, 'I was setting him up so that he would make a bluff.'

Here Tony let the players think that he played like a soggy teabag and been deservedly outdrawn on the river. Setting up the wrong image is an important aspect of the game when you often play in the same school.

SCORECHART

60 Wonderful. I am not sure that I would have achieved this.

50-59 Extremely respectable. Tony made 55 and David 50.

35-49 You may well have lost less than either Tony or I. Danny scored 43.

20-34 This is an unsavoury result.

0-19 A dismal performance.

♣ – ♥ – ♦ – ♠ – ♣ – ♥ – ♦ – ♠

ANSWERS AND ANALYSIS

Holding: 9♥-9♣.

Answer 1: (a) 3 (b) 1 (c) 4 (d) 10.

According to Dr Mahmood Mahmood, statistically this hand is winning against six opponents about half the time. If you are frightened of a raise, then you should obey the dictum, 'If you can't stand the heat, get out of the kitchen.' In tournament play, there is an argument that you should never limp in with the hope of seeing the flop cheaply. If someone raises after you then you usually end up passing, and more chips have gone down the tube. This flaunts the law of conservation of chips. In a cash game, of course, that law does not apply.

Flop: J♥-7♠-3♦.

Answer 2: (a) 0 (b) 1 (c) 5 (d) 10.

Boris did not act aggressively before the pot. Thus Tony is probably winning, unless Boris has a jack in his hand. A check will prove nothing, and may simply give our Russian friend a free card. A £20 bet would suggest that we are not in love with the flop. Since that is indeed the case, why tell the truth? However, a £100 bet might convey the idea that we have a pair higher than jacks, which is quite a nice idea.

Turn: J♥-7♠-3♦-8♣.

Answer 3: (a) 10 (b) 4 (c) 0 (d) 0.

Boris would not have called with just two overcards, so he is most likely winning. The best play is to check.

Answer 4: (a) 10 (b) 5 (c) 0 (d) 6.

Why has Boris bet so little? Is he frightened of your hand? In that case, a robust raise might do the trick. If you are thinking along the lines that you can represent a straight because you have the two nines as blockers, then you are probably more of an Omaha player. If he is very strong, then it would actually be a disaster for you to raise. You cannot stand the action, and will miss out on a possible opportunity to improve. A ten will surely give you the best hand, and it is also probable that a nine will be good enough. Six wins out of 46 is not good enough to give you pot odds, but the implied odds are quite attractive in this situation. The most prudent course is to fold, however.

Answer 5: (a) 10 (b) 5 (c) 2.

It hardly seems likely that any normal hand like A-J will call a pot-sized bet here. Thus it is probably more profitable to check and let Boris take the initiative. Of course, it will be very sad if he just checks it back, but you have been very lucky to fluke the nine.

Answer 6: (a) -5 (b) 10 (c) 2 (d) 6.

With which hands can Boris bet where he will call a raise? Trips or J-10 are the only likely possibilities. That small bet on the turn was very suspicious, and we are generally wary of Boris. A call is in order.

Hand 48

Having a good Time

INTRODUCTION

The game was £5-£10 blinds. Alan held 4♠-4♣ in seat 4, the under the gun player having already passed. There was ample money on the table.

THE PLAY

Question 1: Should Alan: (a) pass (b) call (c) raise £10 (d) raise £30?

(a) ☐	(b) ☐	(c) ☐	(d) ☐	Points: ....

Action: Alan raised £10 and Cyril called, as did Felix after him. Larry then raised a further £10 in the small blind and the big blind folded. The pot was £100 and it was £10 to Alan.

Question 2: Should Alan: (a) pass (b) call (c) raise £10 (d) raise £20 (e) raise £110?

(a) ☐	(b) ☐	(c) ☐	(d) ☐	(e) ☐	Points: ....

Action: Alan called £10, as did Cyril and Felix.

Flop: 10♠-10♦-4♦. Alan held 4♠-4♣. Larry bet £100, so the pot now stood at £230.

Question 3: Should Alan: (a) pass (b) call (c) raise £100 (d) raise £330?

(a) ☐	(b) ☐	(c) ☐	(d) ☐	Points: ....

Action: Alan raised £300. Astonishingly, first Cyril now raised £1000 and then Felix raised a further £2000 all-in. Larry now decided to cut his losses and passed. The pot stood at £5430. It was £3000 for Alan to call, and Cyril would have an additional £2000 if he were to decide to call Felix's £2000 re-raise.

Question 4: Should Alan: (a) pass (b) call (c) raise £2000 all-in on the side?

(a) ☐	(b) ☐	(c) ☐	Points: ....

Action: Alan called, as did Cyril.

Turn: 10♠-10♦-4♦-7♦. Alan held 4♠-4♣. The pot stood at £10,430 and there was £2000 to bet to make a side pot between Alan and Cyril.

Question 5: Should Alan: (a) check (b) bet £2000 all-in?

(a) ☐	(b) ☐	Points: ....

Action: Alan bet £2000 all-in and Cyril called.

River: 10♠-10♦-4♦-7♦-8♥. Alan held 4♠-4♣. There was £10,430 in the main pot and £4000 in the side pot. Alan showed down his hand and scooped the lot. Felix told the table that he had K-10, while Cyril said that, at any rate, he was beating that with A-10. Larry snarled that they were both in terrible shape, as he had passed A-K. We will never know the truth.

Question 6: Assuming both were telling the truth, should Felix have: (a) passed (b) called (c) raised all-in?

(a) ☐	(b) ☐	(c) ☐	Points: ....

Question 7: When Cyril faced the raise from Felix after Alan had already called, should he: (a) pass (b) call (c) raise £2000 all-in?

(a) ☐	(b) ☐	(c) ☐	Points: ....
			Total: ....

SCORECHART

70 This was David's mark. It is an easy score to make.

60-69 You did well on this occasion. Alan scored 47/50.

45-59 A little frayed at the edges. Danny made 58.

30-44 Did you have a rough night?

15-29 Oh well, back to the drawing board.

0-14 You need to go to the poker hospital.

ANSWERS AND ANALYSIS

Holding: 4♠-4♣.

Answer 1: (a) 10 (b) 7 (c) 4 (d) 0.

With seven other players still to act action, there is no reason to think this is even the best made hand. Anyone with two overcards is not be much of an underdog to Alan's hand. The only reason for a call is the hope of improving to trips on the flop, but this happens only around 12% of the time. It is no good considering the likelihood of hitting the trip fours by the river, since Alan is never going to survive that long if he misses on the flop. The only real justification for calling is the implied odds of winning money when you do connect. Although it is often best to fold, limping in is still quite reasonable.

Alternatively you could try a tiny raise of £10. This is not exactly a gay raise, since you are not reopening the betting. It may be enough to inhibit some other players from reraising. If you try either of these ploys, then you should also occasionally do exactly the same thing with a hand with which you intend to reraise. Otherwise, you will become very predictable and your opponents will beat up on you.

In both cases, you should not employ these tactics where you have only a relatively small amount of money on the table, since you would then be disobeying the law of conservation of chips. You really need twenty times what a further raise will cost you. Thus, if the next raise could be £100, you need £2000 in your tank so that you can call the raise.

Answer 2: (a) -5 (b) 10 (c) 1 (d) 0 (e) 0.

Alan is now getting his odds to call, since Larry is playing silly beggars. That is a quintessential gay raise. Should Alan raise a further £10, it is actually more likely that Cyril and Felix will fold than if he were to raise £100. Players do not like being taken for a ride like this with small raises being swapped back and forth. In a limit game, the maximum number of raises in a multi-way pot is typically three or four. In pot-limit there is no knowing when the reraising will stop. However, Alan does not have the type of hand where he wants to reduce the field. He wants to keep the other players in with this kind of drawing hand.

Flop: 10♠-10♦-4♦.

Answer 3: (a) -5 (b) 3 (c) 1 (d) 10.

Alan has hit the virtual crown jewels, so now comes the matter of making the most of his good fortune. A call will set off warning bells among good players. Calling here would be a sign of greater strength than raising would. What could he possible be calling with? Surely it must be either a ten or pocket fours? The only other possibility is a pair of jacks, since he would surely have reraised before the flop with pocket aces, kings or queens. But, if Alan raises then it may possibly appear that he is just trying to take the pot away from Larry. The pair of tens on board is the best possible flop for Alan's pair of fours, since a ten is the most likely card to be held by someone who limped in before the flop. The act of raising may bring the pot to a premature end, but probably so would calling. Whenever you have hit a Weapon of Mass Destruction, you must decide whether or not to slowplay it. Aggression will almost always lead to either a small return or a massive one.

Answer 4: (a) -5 (b) 10 (c) 8.

It is wildly improbable that either player has a full house or quads. But if one has, then you must live and die with this hand. Another all-in raise may cause Cyril to review the situation. You do not want Cyril to pass, although he could still outdraw you if he has, say, A-10.

Turn: 10♠-10♦-4♦-7♦.

Answer 5: (a) 0 (b) 10.

There is no getting away from this hand. Should it turn out that Felix is winning, Alan can still recover something from the wreckage by winning the side pot. Of course, if Cyril is winning, well, goodnight and hope to have sweet dreams! It is even possible that Cyril called on the flop to make a flush. By the same token, he may believe that this is Alan's holding.

Answer 6: (a) 10 (b) 0 (c) -2.

This is one of those rare occasions when you should get away from trips. Felix faced a pot of £2030 and it was £1400 for him to call. Either Alan or Cyril almost certainly has him beaten at this stage of the hand. Given the hands that we actually know are out against him, it is about 7/1 against his improving by the river, so the pot odds are just not there for him to continue in the hand.

Answer 7: (a) 2 (b) 0 (c) 10.

In Omaha we are used to this shell game. One opponent has fours full and the other a ten. Cyril was facing a pot of £8430 and it was £2000 to call or £4000 to raise. Cyril has a draw for nothing provided that it is Felix rather than Alan who has the made full house. Calling was precisely wrong and Cyril should pass or raise the £2000 all-in. As it happens, it makes absolutely no difference to Alan.

Hand 49

How far should one go?

INTRODUCTION

In this game the blinds were £10-£20. Ann had limped in from seat 4 and everyone else had passed so far. I was in seat 8 with Q♦-10♠. The button did not seem to be stirring himself, but this often means very little, since some players only make a decision when it is their turn to act. The pot was £50 and it was £20 to me.

THE PLAY

Question 1: Should I: (a) pass (b) call (c) raise £20 (d) raise £70?

(a) ☐	(b) ☐	(c) ☐	(d) ☐	Points: ....

Action: I made it £80 to go, a raise of £60. This is a bit frisky, but Ann can sometimes be bullied. Everyone passed to Ann, who called. So far, so good!

Flop: A♠-J♦-4♥. I held Q♦-10♠ and the pot was £190. Ann checked.

Question 2: Should I: (a) check (b) bet £50 (c) bet £190?

(a) ☐	(b) ☐	(c) ☐	Points: ....

Action: I bet £150 and Ann called.

Turn: A♠-J♦-4♥-6♥. I held Q♦-10♠ and there was £490 in the pot. Ann checked.

Question 3: Should I: (a) check (b) bet £150 (c) bet £490?

(a) ☐	(b) ☐	(c) ☐	Points: ....

Action: I bet £400. I actually have even fewer nut outs now, since the K♥ could possibly give Ann a flush, but it is still comforting that I have something in my bag of tricks. Ann called.

River: A♠-J♦-4♥-6♥-9♣. I held Q♦-10♠ and the pot was £1290. Ann checked.

Question 4: Should I: (a) check (b) bet £400 (c) bet £1290?

(a) ☐	(b) ☐	(c) ☐	Points: ....
			Total: ....

Action: I checked and displayed the mess I had got myself into. You may as well maximise your advertising. Once a century your opponent will misinterpret the board and muck the winning hand. Ann looked cross-eyed and displayed her hand: Q♥-10♥. We split the pot. I had got away with blue murder – or had she?

Of course, had either of us played more aggressively, we would have won the entire prize, but it is easy to be wise after the event.

SCORECHART

40 You chose a better mix of aggression and defence than I did.

30-39 I scored 36 and Danny made 31.

20-29 Mediocre. David scored 24.

2-19 What type of poker player are you?

ANSWERS AND ANALYSIS

Holding: Q♦-10♠.

Answer 1: (a) 4 (b) 10 (c) 0 (d) 8.

This is not much of a hand, but my position is good. It seems silly to re-open the betting for Ann with a gay raise. However, if you are an inveterate limper, money often seems just to trickle through your fingers.

Flop: A♠-J♦-4♥.

Answer 2: (a) 3 (b) 0 (c) 10.

You should nearly always fire a second shot in this kind of situation, since the flop may have missed your opponent completely. I like to have a chance of winning even when I am bluffing, and here any king gives me the nuts. But you also know that I do not like re-opening the betting when I have a good drawing hand, since I am afraid of being taken off my draw by a raise. Here that is of little concern. It is 11/1 against making the straight next card, so my chances of improving are fairly slim anyhow.

Turn: A♠-J♦-4♥-6♥.

Answer 3: (a) 10 (b) 0 (c) 8.

I can still hope to be able to bully Ann. She probably has an ace with a bad kicker. A small bet will achieve nothing.

River: A♠-J♦-4♥-6♥-9♣.

Answer 4: (a) 10 (b) 2 (c) 7.

Ann has been very stubborn, so surely she is prepared to call one final bet? Some might feel that it is obligatory to bet here, since otherwise I am simply giving up the pot. Some players might also try a small bet, hoping to appear as if they are begging for a call. The decision rests with the moment and the opponent. It is impossible to make a definitive assessment within the confines of a book.

Hand 50

Play the Man, not the Cards

INTRODUCTION

Let us indulge in the fantasy that you are playing against poker legend Doyle Brunson. Presumably you have realised that some of the preceding hands have also been created specifically for this book, but I hope you are not entirely sure which ones.

The first question to be asked is, 'What are you doing playing at the same table as Doyle?' Why bother to confront him, when there are easier fish to fry? I have played against Doyle, and also that other legend, the late Stu Ungar. Indeed, I had to go all the way to Vegas before I could be regarded as 'big' Stew! We played limit seven-card stud, which was much more my scene than theirs.

Clearly we must treat Doyle with a great deal of respect. He has been playing professional poker much longer than I have, and made much more money out of it. On the other hand, he is going to have to play our game, pot-limit, a game somewhat different from no-limit. Also, we have reaped the benefit of having the opportunity to read *Super/System*. This classic book was first published in 1978, and many players have taken its lessons to heart and been successful as a result. No doubt Doyle has moved on from those days. In any case, some of his statements in *Super/System* can be taken with a pinch of salt (for example, he states that he never plays A-Q and loves low suited connectors). Since it is our fantasy hand, we will freeze him in time 25 years ago.

Even so, I doubt whether one aspect of his play has changed much. He likes being a 'boss' player. Players of this nature always want to be the centre of attention and the one making all the moves.

The blinds in this game are \$100-\$200 blinds. The buy-in is \$2000, but everyone has considerably more than that. I doubt that he would play this small, but I did not fancy typing in all those zeros.

The player in seat 3 had passed, and Doyle had raised to \$800 from the fourth seat. Everyone else had passed to you in seat 7, holding **J♠-J♥**. There was \$1100 in the pot and it was \$800 to you.

THE PLAY

Question 1: Should you: (a) pass (b) call (c) raise $800 (d) raise $1900?

(a) ☐	(b) ☐	(c) ☐	(d) ☐	Points: ....

Action: You call and everyone else passes. Alone at last! What a peculiar ambitions against an opponent who is so experienced. Could it be a little like 'shoot-out at high noon'? Please don't let your ego get in the way of the basic objective of winning money.

Flop: Q♠-6♥-2♣. You hold J♠-J♥. Doyle now bets the pot, $1900. We would have been a little surprised if he had bet a lesser figure at this stage of his career. What else would a no-limit player do? I am concealing nothing from you. Now the pot is $3800 and it is $1900 to you.

Question 2: Should you: (a) pass (b) call (c) raise $1900 (d) raise $5700?

(a) ☐	(b) ☐	(c) ☐	(d) ☐	Points: ....

Action: You call.

Turn: Q♠-6♥-2♣-4♦. You hold J♠-J♥. Doyle again bets the pot, $5700. The pot stands at $11,400 and you have $21,000 left.

Question 3: Should you: (a) pass (b) call (c) raise $15,300 all-in?

(a) ☐	(b) ☐	(c) ☐	Points: ....

Hypothetical Turn: Q♠-6♥-2♣-5♦. You hold J♠-J♥. Yet again Doyle bets $5700, making the pot $11,400. You still have $21,000 left.

Question 4: Should you: (a) pass (b) call (c) raise $15,300 all-in?

(a) ☐	(b) ☐	(c) ☐	Points: ....
			Total: ....

Action: In the actual hand, you raise $15,300 all-in. Doyle considers for a moment and then throws in his hand. Old-fashioned boss players do not like to have the initiative taken away from them.

You do not have to play this way against players of this nature. If you play defensively, you may make more profit, and perhaps even win more than they do. But a defensive strategy won't get you the gravy at the end of a tournament or when you are forced to play a series of pots against such an opponent.

SCORECHART

40 Excellent. You are not a mouse. I did not award myself a score, as I knew how the pot was going to turn out. That is not true of all the pots I invented. Some of them quite surprised me!

30-39 There is nothing wrong with that. Circumspect play is more professional.

20-29 Probably a bit weak-kneed. David only made 26 and Danny 24.

10-19 Don't challenge Doyle to a heads-up contest.

2-9 On the other hand, do challenge me to one!

ANSWERS AND ANALYSIS

Holding: J♠-J♥.

Answer 1: (a) -2 (b) 10 (c) 1 (d) 2.

You have a pretty good hand, but do you really want to go bust right away? There are four other players still to act, any one of whom might have something to say about this hand.

Flop: Q♠-6♥-2♣.

Answer 2: (a) 5 (b) 10 (c) 4 (d) 8.

Of course, your hand is totally unrelated to the flop, but that will normally also be true for your opponent. A raise has to be a pretty good percentage play against a strong, aggressive opponent. However, against a weak opponent it could be disastrous. If such a player bets, he very likely has a good hand. There is nothing wrong with passing your pair of jacks, but you want to make a stand. Why not call and let Doyle bury himself? You call.

Answer 3: (a) 6 (b) 0 (c) 10.

Answer 4: (a) 10 (b) 0 (c) 4.

The 4♦ is not a dangerous card at all. Doyle is unlikely to have raised with 6-4 or 5-3. But he could have raised with 4-3 or 6-5. With the 5♦ on the turn it has all become a lot more dangerous. In any case, he may be beating you with any queen or a pair of aces or kings or trips. Of course, we 'know' that he does not play A-Q. After all, we trust *Super/System* like the bible!

Hand 51

Be circumspect

INTRODUCTION

The game was £10-£20 blinds. Alf and Jason had both called for £20. Stan held K♠-J♦ in the 6 seat. The pot stood at £70 and it was £20 to play.

THE PLAY

Question 1: Should Stan: (a) pass (b) call (c) raise £20 (d) raise £100?

(a) ☐	(b) ☐	(c) ☐	(d) ☐	Points: ....

Action: Stan called and Joe also called in seat 8. The small blind made it up to £20 and the big blind checked.

Flop: J♠-9♣-4♥. Stan held K♠-J♦. Both blinds checked and Alf bet £120, causing Jason to pass. The pot was now £240.

Question 2: Should Stan: (a) pass (b) call (c) raise £120 (d) raise £360?

(a) ☐	(b) ☐	(c) ☐	(d) ☐	Points: ....

Action: Stan and then Joe called. Both blinds passed.

Turn: J♠-9♣-4♥-6♥. Stan held K♠-J♦. Alf bet the pot, £480.

Question 3: Should Stan: (a) pass (b) call (c) raise £480 (d) raise £1400?

(a) ☐	(b) ☐	(c) ☐	(d) ☐	Points: ....

Action: Stan called and Joe passed.

River: J♠-9♣-4♥-6♥-6♠. Stan held K♠-J♦. Alf checked. There was £1440 in the pot and Alf had £1500 in chips.

Question 4: Should Stan: (a) check (b) bet £500 (c) bet £1400?

(a) ☐	(b) ☐	(c) ☐	Points: ....

Action: Stan bet £500. In his fine book, *Championship No-Limit and Pot-Limit Hold'em*, T.J. Cloutier states that he always bets the pot (admittedly he is mainly writing about tournament play here). His reasoning is that by varying the size of your bet you may be giving away too much information. This has a considerable measure of truth. Thus, if you do vary the amount of your bets and raises, you must also vary your reasons for your decision. On this occasion, you might have played nines full in the same way as K-J. The truth is that Stan was thirsty for a call from a pair of jacks with an inferior kicker.

If this had been a tournament, and £500 represented a high proportion of your chips, then you would have been more likely to check. On the other hand, if it were a low proportion of your stack, but a big chunk of your opponent's, then you would have been more likely to bet.

Hypothetical Action: Stan bets £500 and Alf raises £1000 all-in. The pot is £3440.

Question 5: Should Stan: (a) pass (b) call?

(a) ☐	(b) ☐	Points: ....
		Total: ....

Returning to reality.

Action: Alf called. It turned out that he held Q♥-J♣. Stan had won a £2440 pot by not playing aggressively. *Super/System* preaches the code that you win the money by taking the initiative. Normally this is true, but not in every case.

SCORECHART

50 My thoughts entirely.

40-49 Very good indeed. David scored 45 and Danny 41.

25-39 Could do better, a great deal better.

15-24 You need to rethink your style.

6-14 Or perhaps a more instinctive approach would be more effective.

ANSWERS AND ANALYSIS

Holding: K♠-J♦.

Answer 1: (a) 10 (b) 7 (c) 0 (d) 1.

This is a very mediocre hand which can often lead to trouble. There are still five people who have not yet acted and the two limpers may be looking for an opportunity to reraise.

Flop: J♠-9♣-4♥.

Answer 2: (a) -1 (b) 10 (c) 0 (d) 5.

Joe has yet to act, so he is a totally unknown quantity at the moment. It is also still possible that one of the blinds may declare war. Also it seems to me this is an example of 'Morton's fork'. If Stan is losing, then he is likely to lose less by not raising. If he is winning, then he is likely to win more by not raising. Of course, he also risks being outdrawn.

Turn: J♠-9♣-4♥-6♥.

Answer 3: (a) 3 (b) 10 (c) 0 (d) 2.

Not much has changed with the extra card on the table. Stan still feels uncomfortable with Joe breathing down his neck.

River: J♠-9♣-4♥-6♥-6♠.

Answer 4: (a) 8 (b) 5 (c) 10.

The choice very much depends on how you got out of bed that morning.

Answer 5: (a) 10 (b) 2.

This is the problem with small raises. Here the reward, if Stan is called and wins the pot, is just £500, whereas the downside is a possible £1500 loss if he is then obliged to call a raise. Alf cannot be bluffing here. If he had wanted to do that, he could have bet £1400 himself, since he could not rely on Stan to bet his hand for him. The only chance for Stan is that his opponent may have overvalued his hand.

Hand 52

Resigning

INTRODUCTION

The game is our standard £10-£20 blinds. Fred was first to call in seat 4. You hold Q♠-J♠ in seat 7. It is £20 to you and the pot is £50.

THE PLAY

Question 1: Should you: (a) pass (b) call (c) raise £20 (d) raise £80?

(a) ☐	(b) ☐	(c) ☐	(d) ☐	Points: ....

Action: You called. The next two players then passed, Cyril called in the small blind, and Bert checked in the big blind.

Flop: K♥-J♦-4♠. You hold Q♠-J♠ and there is £80 in the pot. All three players in front of you check.

Question 2: Should you: (a) check (b) bet £20 (c) bet £80?

(a) ☐	(b) ☐	(c) ☐	Points: ....

Action: You bet £80. Bert and Fred both called.

Turn: K♥-J♦-4♠-8♦. You hold Q♠-J♠ and the pot is £320. Both players check to you.

Question 3: Should you: (a) check (b) bet £80 (c) bet £320?

(a) ☐	(b) ☐	(c) ☐	Points: ....

Action: You check.

River: K♥-J♦-4♠-8♦-8♥. You hold Q♠-J♠ and the pot is still £320. Both players check to you.

Question 4: Should you: (a) check (b) bet £100 (c) bet £320?

(a) ☐	(b) ☐	(c) ☐	Points: ....
			Total: ....

Action: You check. Bert held J♦-4♥ and Fred K♠-9♠. Thus Fred won this small pot. Bert allowed himself to be viciously outdrawn. Apparently he was intending to move in on you if you had bet on the turn, but it is blindingly obvious that Bert and Fred had hands that were beating you. Ironically, had you bet on the river, Fred might have passed with his weak kicker, and you would then have been winning.

SCORECHART

40 Danny's score. Wonderful.

30-49 My score of 38 included the bet on the flop. David scored 34.

20-29 Nothing great.

10-19 Fatally flawed.

0-9 Appallingly bad.

ANSWERS AND ANALYSIS

Holding: Q♠-J♠.

Answer 1: (a) 0 (b) 10 (c) 0 (d) 5.

This is a moderate hand. There are still several players to act. Why stir things up with what is fundamentally a drawing hand?

Flop: K♥-J♦-4♠.

Answer 2: (a) 10 (b) 0 (c) 8.

In small pots such as this one, a check usually means what it says. Few people make fancy plays, so you may well be winning. Why not get the pot over and the next one on the road? You do not have to worry about being raised and having to give up on a pot that you would otherwise have had a good chance to win. Only a jack on the turn will make you feel comfortable so, if you are raised, then you are just going to have to throw in your cards. You still know nothing at all about your opponents' hands. Indeed, Bert's cards are purely random, since he just checked in the big blind.

Turn: K♥-J♦-4♠-8♦.

Answer 3: (a) 10 (b) 0 (c) 1.

Surely at least one opponent has the drop on you? If not, well you are just going to have to risk being outdrawn. Of course, you can fire another shot as a bluff. By all means be my guest. Just don't ask me to back you in a game.

River: K♥-J♦-4♠-8♦-8♥.

Answer 4: (a) 10 (b) 0 (c) 2.

Nobody is likely to believe that pairing the eights has improved your hand.

Hand 53

Adrenaline

INTRODUCTION

The antes were again £10-£20. Art had called under the gun and the next two players had passed. Bill held A♥-J♥ in seat 6. The pot was £50 and it was £20 to play.

THE PLAY

Question 1: Should Bill: (a) pass (b) call (c) raise £20 (d) raise £80?

(a) ☐	(b) ☐	(c) ☐	(d) ☐	Points: ....

Action: Bill made it £100 to go. He was obeying the principle that limping is indeed a limp strategy. Both Jack and Jill called after him. The blinds then folded and Art called the raise.

Flop: 10♥-9♥-4♠. Bill held A♥-J♥ and there was £430 in the pot. Art had only £800 left; the others had £8000 each. Art checked.

Question 2: Should Bill: (a) check (b) bet £100 (c) bet £430?

(a) ☐	(b) ☐	(c) ☐	Points: ....

Action: Bill bet £400, Jack passed and Jill called.

Hypothetical Action: Instead of £800 left, Art has £2500 left and raises the full £1630. The pot is now £3260.

Question 3: Should Bill: (a) pass (b) call (c) raise £1630 (d) raise £4890?

(a) ☐	(b) ☐	(c) ☐	(d) ☐	Points: ....

Returning to the actual hand.

Action: Art raised £400 all-in, bringing the pot up to £2030. Since this was not an under-raise, it reopens the betting for both Bill and Jill.

Question 4: Should Bill: (a) pass (b) call (c) raise £400 (d) raise £2400?

(a) ☐	(b) ☐	(c) ☐	(d) ☐	Points: ....

Action: Bill called.

Hypothetical Action: Jill raises £2830, making the total pot £5660. There would then have been £4370 left to bet.

Question 5: Should Bill: (a) pass (b) call (c) raise £4370 all-in?

(a) ☐	(b) ☐	(c) ☐	Points: ....

Now back to the actual hand.

Action: Anyway, that was all academic, since Jill just called.

Turn: 10♥-9♥-4♠-5♥. Bill held A♥-J♥. The pot stood at £2830 and Art was all-in.

Question 6: Should Bill: (a) check (b) bet £500 (c) bet £1500 (d) bet £2800?

(a) ☐	(b) ☐	(c) ☐	(d) ☐	Points: ....

Action: Bill checked and Jill bet £2500. The pot stood at £5330 and there was £4700 left to bet.

Question 7: Should Bill: (a) pass (b) call (c) raise £2500 (d) raise £4700 all-in?

(a) ☐	(b) ☐	(c) ☐	(d) ☐	Points: ....
				Total: ....

Action: Bill raised £4700 all-in and Jill called.

River: 10♥-9♥-4♠-5♥-6♥. Bill held A♥-J♥. The main pot stood at £2830 and the side pot at £14,400. As Jill called, she said, 'I'm not drawing dead if you have the nut flush.' As the 6♥ hit the table, Bill let out a tremendous cry of anguish. He thought that Jill had made a straight flush. In fact she held K♥-Q♥, so that Bill had won the pot. Art showed down his 10♠-9♦. Jill was actually drawing dead, of course, because the J♥ was in Bill's hand. Art sulkily exclaimed, 'They didn't even have to wait a card to hit their flushes!'

We thought Bill was going to suffer a heart attack from this incident. He certainly got his money's worth in adrenaline rush. Since I wasn't involved the pot, I had completely forgotten this incident until the following hand brought it flooding back.

I was playing Omaha against Lettuce (who features in my book on Omaha). On the flop I had the nut flush and all the money went in. As it did so, he echoed exactly what Jill had said years earlier. 'I'm not drawing dead if you have the nut flush.' Again a possible straight flush came on the river and this time he made it and beat me in my biggest pot of the day. Of course, I thought he meant that he not only had a flush but also had trips. Outdraws are much more common in Omaha, and I didn't sulk for more than a couple of minutes.

Jill lost a very large sum of money in the pot, but it is not clear whether she made a mistake at any stage. There was nothing wrong with calling before the flop. On the flop she held a flush draw, two overcards and a middle-pin straight flush draw. She was not to know that Bill's hand dominated hers at this point. Nor was there anything wrong with betting the hand on the turn, although by betting less than the pot she could have left herself more reason to pass a raise.

Perhaps she could have passed the all-in raise on the turn. If Bill is bluffing with the bare A♥ and she passes, his only reward might be the side pot of £2500, since Art may have him beaten in the main pot. Thus it is a less likely bluff, unless Bill knows that Jill is a good enough player to realise this and will therefore pass. But surely this is taking the existential nature of a bluff in poker too far?

But what if she had raised on the flop at her first opportunity? You will have noted that Bill felt much less comfortable when put under pressure. It is quite possible that he would have passed. The fly in the ointment is that Art's call might have given him adequate equity. He would be laying out £1230 to win £3260, with implied odds of winning more money from Jill.

What if she had raised at her second opportunity on the flop? Well, that might have worked. Had Bill passed, he would have found out that he had missed out on a pot he would have won. This might have enraged him, and then the game would really have been on.

Should we have any sympathy for Art who, after all, had the best hand on the flop? None whatsoever. Out of position, he should have passed for the first £20, and calling the £80 pre-flop raise served merely to compound the error. It turned out that he needed about 30 times this sum to protect his hand on the flop. He was under-funded for a drawing hand.

This hand demonstrates that it is essential to have adequate funds for your play, and that aggression usually pays off.

SCORECHART

70 Truly great. Please do not play against me. David managed this result.

60-69 An excellent result in a difficult hand. Bill scored 68.

45-59 Satisfactory. The decisions were on a knife-edge.

30-44 Reread this chapter. Danny only scored 47.

15-29 An uncomfortable result.

0-14 You have yet to get to grips with the basics of poker.

ANSWERS AND ANALYSIS

Holding: A♥-J♥.

Answer 1: (a) 0 (b) 10 (c) 0 (d) 8.

In pot-limit hold'em, there is much more emphasis on pairs than there is in the limit form of the game. There are still three players to act, plus the two unknown quantities in the blinds. Thus it becomes a borderline decision whether to call or raise.

Flop: 10♥-9♥-4♠.

Answer 2: (a) 5 (b) 2 (c) 10.

This pot is motoring along nicely. Bill has an excellent four to a nut flush with two overcards. He can only be an underdog to A-10, J-10, an overpair to the flop, two pair or a set. The best way to make money here is to lead out. Having raised before the flop, most people would bet whatever they held. Thus Bill is giving away very little information by betting. Were he to check and then raise, he would be signalling his hand rather precisely.

Answer 3: (a) 10 (b) 4 (c) -3 (d) -5.

Forget about those overcards, Bill is only going to win with a flush. He is around about 2/1 against making the hand by the river. The pot odds are just not there, because Art still has £470 to bet on the turn. What about the implied odds of Jill calling? What makes you seriously imagine that she will call here? If you do think that she may have an interest in calling, then the worst possible move is to reraise and drive her out. It may break your heart to pass such a fine draw, but don't let it break your bank.

Answer 4: (a) -5 (b) 10 (c) 4 (d) 6.

Bill certainly has pot odds here, so it would be insane to pass. Since he has a drawing hand, why frighten off Jill, who is certain to call if he doesn't raise? Yes, well, read on.

Answer 5: (a) 10 (b) 8 (c) 8.

This is a completely different scenario from that if Art had been able to make a pot raise and have money left, as in Question 3. Why would Jill just call the first time around and now want to make a full-blooded raise? Surely she could not have been relying on Art's raise to reopen the betting? It is just possible that he telegraphed his intentions to her after Bill bet. After all, Bill's attention was directed towards Jack and Jill, who were to his left. He might have missed a nuance by Art who lay to his right.

However, it is much more likely that she has a moderate hand and has been emboldened by the fact that Bill just called Art's £400 raise. For example, she could have 5♥-4♥. In that case she knows that against Bill she has a 'Morton's fork' situation. Either she is winning, or has the best draw. Alternatively, it could be that she has A-10 or 8♥-7♥. In that case she hopes to drive out Bill in case he has the nut flush draw. It is sometimes regarded as unethical to raise in a hand where there is no side pot and you know that you are losing to the all-in player. Here that philosophy would be plainly wrong.

There is no correct answer to this problem. I was actually inclined to award ten points for each decision!

Turn: 10♥-9♥-4♠-5♥.

Answer 6: (a) 10 (b) 4 (c) 0 (d) 3.

A warm glow has come over Bill, and he must now make the most of his good fortune. It is most unlikely that Jill has trips, since she should have raised on the flop with such a hand. Bill can only hope for another unlikely possibility: that Jill has also made a flush. The problem with betting out here is that it cannot really be a bluff. The all-in player must have some type of hand, so what is Bill betting with to create a new side pot?

Answer 7: (a) -5 (b) 2 (c) 0 (d) 10.

Here Bill's raise could be a bluff, since there is now the side pot to win. From Jill's viewpoint he could perhaps have A♥-A♦, and be semi-bluffing with the nut flush draw. With good reason people seldom believe that their opponents also have flushes. The problem with calling is that another heart might show up on the river, destroying the action. An open pair might also have the same effect.

Hand 54

Just play it cool

INTRODUCTION

The game was the usual $10-$20 blinds. Al had raised to $60 in seat 4 and Ian had called. I was in seat 7 with 7♠-7♦. It was $60 to me and the pot was $150.

THE PLAY

Question 1: Should I: (a) pass (b) call (c) raise $60 (d) raise $210?

(a) ☐ (b) ☐ (c) ☐ (d) ☐ Points: ....

Action: I called, as did Ed in seat 9. The small blind passed, but Owen also called in the big blind.

Flop: 9♠-8♥-6♣. I held 7♠-7♦. The pot was $310.

Hypothetical Action: Owen and Al check. Ian then bets $300, so the pot is $610.

Question 2: Should I: (a) pass (b) call (c) raise $300 (d) raise $900?

(a) ☐ (b) ☐ (c) ☐ (d) ☐ Points: ....

Returning to the actual hand.

Action: Owen checked, Al bet $100 and Ian passed. The pot was now $410.

Question 3: Should I: (a) pass (b) call (c) raise $100 (c) raise $500?

(a) ☐ (b) ☐ (c) ☐ Points: ....

Action: I raised $400. Ed passed, Owen called and Al passed.

Turn: 9♠-8♥-6♣-4♣. I held 7♠-7♦ and the pot was $1410. Owen checked.

Question 4: Should I: (a) check (b) bet $500 (c) bet $1400?

(a) ☐ (b) ☐ (c) ☐ Points: ....

Action: I checked. Some may call that pusillanimous (if they can pronounce it, let alone spell it!), but I call it circumspect.

River: 9♠-8♥-6♣-4♣-K♦. I held 7♠-7♦ and there was still $1410 in the pot. Owen checked.

Question 5: Should I: (a) check (b) bet $500 (c) bet $1400?

(a) ☐	(b) ☐	(c) ☐	Points: ....
			Total: ....

Action: I checked. Owen held A♣-7♣ and thus I won the pot. Later that evening he mentioned to me that had I bet on the turn, he was intending to raise and try to take the pot away from me, having made a backdoor flush draw. Well, it is easy to talk after the event. So, I gave him a free card when he had six cards to split the pot and 12 ways to win the pot, two of which could have seriously damaged my bankroll. We're none of us perfect.

SCORECHART

50 Copycat. Don't be smug. Others would play this differently.

40-49 A normal, excellent score. David scored 44.

25-39 This might well have led to a bleak evening. Danny scored 32.

10-24 I will not be backing you in a poker game.

0-9 Continue practising on the Internet with play money for the time being.

ANSWERS AND ANALYSIS

Holding: 7♠-7♦.

Answer 1: (a) 0 (b) 10 (c) 0 (d) 0.

It is okay to call the raise here, since I have a good position. Some people may attach some type of significance to the fact I had a pair of sevens in seat 7. If that is their bag, lead on.

Flop: 9♠-8♥-6♣.

Answer 2: (a) 10 (b) 5 (c) -5 (d) 4.

This is an excellent drawing hand, but I do not like to be a caller. Even if a ten comes, I will not make the nuts. This is not the way to get rich, since Ian could be betting with Q-J. Also, you have to consider all those other players in the pot, who may still spring to life with a raise. A small raise would be crazy here, leading me into territory that I have no wish to explore.

Answer 3: (a) 0 (b) 8 (c) 2 (d) 10.

Al's bet looks more like a question mark than a real lead into the pot. He raised before the flop and now feels mandated to act. A raise may win it here and now.

Turn: 9♠-8♥-6♣-4♣.

Answer 4: (a) 10 (b) 0 (c) 6.

You have not met him before, but Owen can be a rough, tough player. He is no easy customer. It is better to go quietly into the good night, or hope that the pair is winning. If I bet, there is no way that I can stand a raise.

River: 9♠-8♥-6♣-4♣-K♦.

Answer 5: (a) 10 (b) 2 (c) 0.

I was all at sea, with no idea what he could possibly be holding. Why should a king have helped my hand? If he is winning, he will call and, if he is losing he can either pass or raise and try to take the pot away from me. Moreover, here he would be successful with a raise.

Hand 55

Get on with it

INTRODUCTION

The game was the familiar £10-£20 blinds. Ray held A♣-6♣ under the gun in seat 3.

THE PLAY

Question 1: Should Ray: (a) pass (b) call (c) raise £20 (d) raise £50?

(a) ☐	(b) ☐	(c) ☐	(d) ☐	Points: ....

Action: Ray called and three players limped in after him. The small blind passed and the big blind checked.

Flop: 9♠-6♦-2♣. Ray held A♣-6♣ and the pot was £110 with five players still in. The original big blind checked.

Question 2: Should Ray: (a) check (b) bet £20 (c) bet £70 (d) bet £110?

(a) ☐	(b) ☐	(c) ☐	(d) ☐	Points: ....

Action: Ray checked and the other three players did likewise.

Turn: 9♠-6♦-2♣-A♠. Ray held A♣-6♣. The pot was still £110 and once again the original big blind checked.

Question 3: Should Ray: (a) check (b) bet £20 (c) bet £70 (d) bet £110?

(a) ☐	(b) ☐	(c) ☐	(d) ☐	Points: ....

Action: Ray checked and so did everyone else.

River: 9♠-6♦-2♣-A♠-J♣. Ray held A♣-6♣ and there was still £110 in the pot. The first player now checked for a third time.

Question 4: Should Ray: (a) check (b) bet £20 (c) bet £70 (d) bet £110?

(a) ☐	(b) ☐	(c) ☐	(d) ☐	Points: ....

Action: Ray bet £75. At last, a decision with which we can agree. Everyone passed to Harold, one of the original limpers, who now raised £250. The big blind lost no time in releasing his cards, since Harold has a reputation as a very tight player. It is said that he last bluffed when the old queen died. That, of course, was Queen Victoria. All this is very unfair. Actually he calls fairly frequently, but never raises without a cast-iron certainty.

The pot was £510 and it was £250 to Ray.

Question 5: Should he: (a) pass (b) call (c) raise £250 (d) raise £750?

(a) ☐	(b) ☐	(c) ☐	(d) ☐	Points: ....
				Total: ....

Action: As I am sure you expected, Ray called. Harold turned over his pair of jacks in the hole and thus won a £760 pot. Ray had contrived to lose a small pot, rather than win an even smaller one.

Many players dislike playing at the same table as Harold. They feel that he is just taking up an empty seat in which a live one could be ensnared. There is some truth in that, but he is an overall loser, albeit at a very slow rate. The real problem is that the other players do not want to give him action, and any time he enters the fray the pots are therefore smaller than they would be for anyone else.

SCORECHART

50 You understand this game.

40-49 A very good score. David scored 44 and Danny 40.

30-39 A rather wretched result.

20-29 Ray scored 23.

1-29 In its own way, a splendid achievement.

ANSWERS AND ANALYSIS

Holding: A♣-6♣.

Answer 1: (a) 10 (b) 3 (c) 0 (d) 0.

There are eight opponents left who may raise and you have bad position. Of course, we would be astonished if Ray, who we have met before, were to pass in this situation.

Flop: 9♠-6♦-2♣.

Answer 2: (a) 6 (b) 2 (c) 10 (d) 7.

It is entirely possible that this hand is winning. Even if it is not, then you are unlikely to be raised except by a very strong hand. You have five good outs (three aces and two sixes) against a player with just a nine in his hand.

Turn: 9♠-6♦-2♣-A♠.

Answer 3: (a) 2 (b) 0 (c) 6 (d) 10.

It is almost certain that Ray is winning here. It is therefore essential to clear out at least some of the players who might be able to draw out on him. If you checked, intending to raise if someone else had bet, then score an extra two points. But that is rather grudging, as it is not the optimum play. A hand such as A-10 may well call you here, but it is not going to initiate the betting.

River: 9♠-6♦-2♣-A♠-J♣.

Answer 4: (a) 4 (b) 4 (c) 10 (d) 4.

Ray should still be winning, but there is always some danger with four opponents in the pot. Betting a moderate amount to win some loose change seems to be the best policy here.

Answer 5: (a) 10 (b) 0 (c) -5 (d) 1.

The odds against Harold having made his first loose play of the 21st century are rather long. If you fancy a long-shot, you could try raising, since Harold probably only has trip jacks and could conceivably pass, fearing trip aces. If you think he is that bad a player, just try it some time. He is well aware that Ray would very likely have raised before the flop with pocket aces and, if not, at least have bet out on the flop.

Hand 56

Life can be very unfair

INTRODUCTION

This hand was the familiar £10-£20 blinds. Alf had called in seat 3 and the next player had folded. Ray held 8♠-7♣ in seat 5. The pot was £50 and it was £20 to call. Among the players still to act was Fiery in seat 8.

THE PLAY

Question 1: Should Ray: (a) pass (b) call (c) raise £20 (d) raise £80?

(a) ☐	(b) ☐	(c) ☐	(d) ☐	Points: ....

Action: Ray committed a cardinal sin here by calling. Why does this come as no surprise from him? The notion that this is only £20, so what does it matter, is completely fallacious. Big pots grow from small bets.

The next two players called and Fiery raised £130. The blinds passed and Alf called. The pot was £390.

Question 2: Should Ray: (a) pass (b) call (c) raise £130 (d) raise £520?

(a) ☐	(b) ☐	(c) ☐	(d) ☐	Points: ....

Action: Ray called, as did the other two players.

Flop: 9♦-8♣-7♥. Ray held 8♠-7♣. Alf now checked. The pot was £780.

Question 3: Should Ray: (a) check (b) bet £100 (c) bet £300 (d) bet £780?

(a) ☐	(b) ☐	(c) ☐	(d) ☐	Points: ....

Action: Ray bet £535. I doubt even he knew why he had chosen such an odd sum. The next two players passed, Fiery called and Alf passed. So far, so good. Ray is isolated with the other loose player and he can continue to play poker.

Turn: 9♦-8♣-7♥-7♦. Ray held 8♠-7♣. The pot was £1850 with £7000 left to bet.

Question 4: Should Ray: (a) check (b) bet £600 (c) bet £1000 (d) bet £1800?

(a) ☐	(b) ☐	(c) ☐	(d) ☐	Points: ....

Action: Ray checked and Fiery bet £1800. The pot was £3650 and there was £5200 left with which to raise.

Question 5: Should Ray: (a) pass (b) call (c) raise £1800 (d) raise £5200 all-in?

(a) ☐	(b) ☐	(c) ☐	(d) ☐	Points: ....

Action: Ray called.

River: 9♦-8♣-7♥-7♦-A♣. Ray held 8♠-7♣. There was £5450 in the pot with £5200 left to bet.

Question 6: Should Ray: (a) check (b) bet £1800 (c) bet £5200 all-in?

(a) ☐	(b) ☐	(c) ☐	Points: ....
			Total: ....

Action: Ray checked and Fiery also checked, showing his hand, J♦-10♦. Thus Ray won a £5450 pot, although he was outplayed at virtually every stage of the hand. We will never know whether Fiery would have called, had Ray gone all-in on the turn. Fiery was visibly delighted that things weren't worse, since he had avoided going completely belly-up in the pot. We will also never know whether he could have forced Ray out by raising with the nuts on the flop.

Note how much simpler it would have been for Ray to play this pot on the button. Drawing hands are improved enormously by a better position.

SCORECHART

60 I will be very wary if I am ever in a pot against you.

50-59 You deserve a pat on the back. David scored 58.

40-49 Danny scored 46. Well, he is inexperienced.

30-39 Ray scored 32. I would have won nothing.

15-29 Buy more poker books. The money will be going to a good home.

0-14 This is hard to believe.

♣ – ♥ – ♦ – ♠ – ♣ – ♥ – ♦ – ♠

ANSWERS AND ANALYSIS

Holding: 8♠-7♣.

Answer 1: (a) 10 (b) -3 (c) -5 (d) -5.

This would be a dreadful call. The hand is weak and we know that Fiery will probably raise. Alf wasn't born yesterday and he may be intending a reraise.

Answer 2: (a) 10 (b) -1 (c) -5 (d) -5.

This hand is still garbage. Also there are still two players who may decide to reraise.

Flop: 9♦-8♣-7♥.

Answer 3: (a) 0 (b) 2 (c) 5 (d) 10.

This is a good hand, but there are five players in the pot. With such a coordinated board Ray cannot assume that Fiery will bet if everyone else checks. Thus if Ray checks, he may simply be giving everyone a free card. The hand is fraught with danger and Ray does not really want to check and then raise. The pot would then become very big, and Ray will still lack any firm indication of whether he is ahead or behind. Much the best play is to bet and see what happens. A £100 bet is sending a boy on a man's errand, you will be offering excellent pot odds and will learn nothing. Thus the best course is to bet the maximum.

Turn: 9♦-8♣-7♥-7♦.

Answer 4: (a) 10 (b) 0 (c) 4 (d) 8.

Ray has a full house and yet he still does not know where he stands. This seems to be yet another example of 'Morton's fork'. If he is winning, then he is unlikely to be outdrawn. A check may elicit either a bluff from Fiery, or a bet with an inferior hand. A bet may open up a smelly can of worms, but it would have the advantage of clarifying the strength of Fiery's hand.

Answer 5: (a) -3 (b) 6 (c) 0 (d) 10.

You will not get rich in hold'em by finding reasons to pass full houses against loose opponents with a card to come. Ray was now petrified by the situation. Surely Fiery must have a good hand? Again, if Ray is winning now, then he is unlikely to get blown away by the river card. An all-in bet means no more problems, no painful river decision.

River: 9♦-8♣-7♥-7♦-A♣.

Answer 6: (a) 10 (b) 2 (c) 8.

This ace is another scare card. But then, alarm bells have been ringing in our hero's ears throughout this pot.

Hand 57

Ever be a Bettor

INTRODUCTION

The game was £10-£20 blinds. Three people had limped in before the flop. I was in the small blind with Q♣-9♣. Thus it was £10 to me, and the pot stood at £90.

THE PLAY

Question 1: Should I: (a) pass (b) call (c) raise £20 (d) raise £100?

(a) ☐	(b) ☐	(c) ☐	(d) ☐	Points: ....

Action: I called £10. The big blind did not raise.

Flop: A♣-10♦-6♣. I held Q♣-9♣. There was £100 in the pot and four people to act after me.

Question 2: Should I: (a) check (b) bet £20 (c) bet £100?

(a) ☐	(b) ☐	(c) ☐	Points: ....

Action: I bet £100. I would have liked to bet less, perhaps £75, but the most natural movement is to loft in a £100 chip. Nick called.

Hypothetical Action: Ted, the only other player now left, raises £400 on the button.

Question 3: Should I: (a) pass (b) call (c) raise £400 (d) raise £1200?

(a) ☐	(b) ☐	(c) ☐	(d) ☐	Points: ....

Let us return to the actual hand.

Action: I bet £100, and Nick and Ted both called.

Turn: A♣-10♦-6♣-8♥. I held Q♣-9♣ and there was £400 in the pot.

Question 4: Should I: (a) check (b) bet £100 (c) bet £200 (d) bet £400?

(a) ☐	(b) ☐	(c) ☐	(d) ☐	Points: ....

Action: I bet £350. We have discussed this idea before. It is not necessarily a sign of weakness to bet slightly less than the size of the pot. If I held a very strong hand, then I might well give a little tempter like this. I often do.

Nick called, but Ted passed. We each had £4000 left to bet.

Hypothetical River: A♣-10♦-6♣-8♥-3♣. I held Q♣-9♣. There was £1100 in the pot.

Question 5: Should I: (a) check (b) bet £400 (c) bet £1000?

(a) ☐	(b) ☐	(c) ☐	Points: ....

Hypothetical Action: I check and Nick bets £1100. There is £2200 in the pot.

Question 6: Should I: (a) pass (b) call (c) raise £1100 (c) raise £2900 all-in?

(a) ☐	(b) ☐	(c) ☐	Points: ....

Now back to actual hand.

River: A♣-10♦-6♣-8♥-3♥. I held Q♣-9♣. There was £1100 in the pot.

Question 7: Should I: (a) check (b) bet £400 (c) bet £1000?

(a) ☐	(b) ☐	(c) ☐	Points: ....
			Total: ....

Action: I bet £1000. Nick passed, petulantly showing his K♣-7♣ and asking, 'Why can I never hit my hand?' Note that not only did he have the better flush draw than me, but also a nine would even have made him a straight.

I was surprised that such an experienced player would call before the flop with a really weak hand like K♣-7♣. I was also extremely surprised that he called on the turn with only nine apparent outs. I did not show my bluff. In my experience, I can never have enough good hands, so I do not want people to think that I bluff frequently. The way the pot played out, it is hard to believe Nick could or would call at the end with his hand. Even a player with J♣-10♣ was unlikely to have the mindset to call on the river, since people with drawing hands seldom consider a call when they miss. The biggest danger to me was A-X.

SCORECHART

70 A score of which you can be proud. David made top marks.

60-69 Well done. Danny scored 60.

45-59 A bit messy. Were you too defensive?

30-44 Please join our game at the Grosvenor Victoria.

15-29 I can just imagine the scene. You lose another pot and then turn to me and say: 'But I've read all your books!'

2-13 Practice, practice, practice!

ANSWERS AND ANALYSIS

Holding: Q♣-9♣.

Answer 1: (a) 0 (b) 10 (c) 0 (d) 0.

My hand can best be described as mediocre, and I am out of position. Moreover, it can become a trap hand, since I may easily be dominated if either of my cards pairs on the flop. But only the big blind can raise, and 9/1 odds are very tasty, so it is a clear call.

Flop: A♣-10♦-6♣.

Answer 2: (a) 8 (b) 2 (c) 10.

I did not seriously think that I had the best made hand here, but I do have a very good draw, provided that no-one else is drawing to the nut flush. One opponent from hell would hold K♣-J♣, almost completely dominating me so that I can only win with a nine or two running cards. Alternatively, K♣-10♣ would leave me looking for a queen. It is also a hand more likely to raise.

I would hate to check and call with a hand that could be drawing virtually dead, but I am generally prepared to bet with almost anything. The initiative is often enough to make my hand a winner. Nobody showed any interest in getting busy before the flop, so it is unlikely that there are any real monsters coming to savage me.

Answer 3: (a) 10 (b) 3 (c) -2 (d) 4.

I would pass. I am always more comfortable as the aggressor, and I prefer to be in late position when I am drawing. Here my draw is not even to the nuts. Furthermore, I am exposing myself to the possibility of a reraise by Nick.

Turn: A♣-10♦-6♣-8♥.

Answer 4: (a) 7 (b) 0 (c) 4 (d) 10.

My opponents seem appropriately cowed, so I have a good chance of being able to secure the prize right there and then. It is most unlikely that anyone has called to make a middle-pin straight, particularly since I have the 9♣ myself. If a seven comes on the river, this should give me the only straight on the table.

Answer 5: (a) 10 (b) 2 (c) 0.

If I bet, the only hand I am likely to be called by, where I am winning, is something like J♣-10♣. In fact, most players would have raised with that hand on the flop, but perhaps Nick wanted to encourage other callers. If I check, Nick may have the bare K♣ and decide to try to steal the pot with a bet.

Answer 6: (a) 0 (b) 10 (c) 1 (d) 0.

Nick may have a lower flush or he may simply be bluffing. I must make a crying call. If you are convinced that Nick will call a reraise with a losing hand, then you could try raising £1100. This is very risky, since Nick will then be in a position to reraise back, possibly even with the bare K♣. That would cause a headache for which no doctor can prescribe suitable pills.

River: A♣-10♦-6♣-8♥-3♥.

Answer 7: (a) 2 (b) 2 (c) 10.

It would be terribly wet to check now and just give up on the pot. Of course, it is never terrible to stop bluffing, but there are plenty of possible missed draws out there. If you answered (a) here, but (d) in Question 4, then deduct two points.

Hand 58

Have a nice Day

INTRODUCTION

The blinds were again £10-£20. Two players had limped in. Alf held 10♣-8♣ in seat 6. The pot was £70 and it was £20 to play.

THE PLAY

Question 1: Should he: (a) pass (b) call (c) raise £20 (d) raise £100?

(a) ☐	(b) ☐	(c) ☐	(d) ☐	Points: ....

Action: Alf called. In retrospect I was surprised at this play from a fairly tight, orthodox player.

Bert raised £100 in seat 8. Harry in seat 9 called and both blinds passed. One of the two original limpers, Cyril, called as well, so there was £430 in the pot and it was £100 to call. Cyril had just £1000 left on the table, whereas Alf covered the table and the other two players had about £5000 each.

Question 2: Should Alf: (a) pass (b) call (c) raise £100 (d) raise £530?

(a) ☐	(b) ☐	(c) ☐	(d) ☐	Points: ....

Action: Alf called.

Flop: Q♣-9♦-6♠. Alf held 10♣-8♣ and there was £530 in the pot. Cyril checked.

Question 3: Should Alf: (a) check (b) bet £100 (c) bet £350 (d) bet £530?

(a) ☐	(b) ☐	(c) ☐	(d) ☐	Points: ....

Action: Alf bet £400.

Hypothetical Action: Bert raises £1330 and both Harry and Cyril pass. The pot is £2660 and there will still be £3270 left to bet if Alf calls.

Question 4: Should Alf: (a) pass (b) call (c) raise £1330 (d) raise £3270 all-in?

(a) ☐	(b) ☐	(c) ☐	(d) ☐	Points: ....

Back to the actual hand.

Action: Bert called and the other two players both passed.

Turn: Q♣-9♦-6♠-7♥. Alf held 10♣-8♣. The pot was £1330 and there was still £4600 left to bet.

Question 5: Should Alf: (a) check (b) bet £400 (c) bet £1000 (d) bet £1330?

(a) ☐	(b) ☐	(c) ☐	(d) ☐	Points: ....

Action: Alf bet £1000 and Bert raised £3300. The pot was now £6630 and there was still £300 left in play.

Question 6: Should Alf: (a) pass (b) call (c) raise £300 all-in?

(a) ☐	(b) ☐	(c) ☐	Points: ....
			Total: ....

Action: Alf raised £300 all-in and, of course, Bert called. The final pot was £7230.

River: Q♣-9♦-6♠-7♥-A♣. Alf held 10♣-8♣ and Bert Q♠-Q♦. He sat there for some time, dismayed at the injustice of it all. From Alf's viewpoint, it was a pleasant way to finish a book.

SCORECHART

60 Congratulations. If this has been your usual score, you have graduated.

50-59 You have done your teacher proud. David scored 54 and Danny 52.

40-49 Alf scored 35/50. The way things turned out, his play won the most money.

20-39 A very clumsy performance.

0-19 It is often said that things can only get better, but this is one cliché that should simply be ignored – especially by poker players.

ANSWERS AND ANALYSIS

Holding: 10♣-8♣.

Answer 1: (a) 10 (b) 4 (c) 0 (d) 0.

Any straightening hand with a gap is rather like a toothless fairy.

Answer 2: (a) 10 (b) 3 (c) 0 (d) 0.

Nothing has changed, except that the value of Alf's implied odds has diminished sharply. One saving grace is that Alf cannot be reraised, but it is also true that the action so far suggests that the other contestants may hold a number of aces and kings.

Flop: Q♣-9♦-6♠.

Answer 3: (a) 10 (b) 0 (c) 6 (d) 8.

Alf has a double belly-buster straight draw. Although a jack does not give him the nut straight, if he hits his draw, his hand will be hard to read. You know that I prefer to bet out, rather than to check and call. You should build your own style.

You may have already decided to check and pass a bet; or to check and raise a bet. If so, score an extra two points in each case.

Answer 4: (a) 10 (b) 2 (c) 0 (d) 5.

The odds are not good enough for a call. It is true that Alf is only a little worse than 2/1 against making the straight, but that is only if he takes the hand all the way to the river. What about the implied odds if he hits his hand on the turn? In that case, he hopes to win £5930 for an outlay of £1330. This is only 9/2 implied odds, and it is 5/1 against making the straight on the turn. If you ignore simple arithmetic, you will definitely go broke.

The situation favours passing or raising all-in. Unless you are up against trips, raising is not a bad play. It is bluffing with outs. Bert probably has one of A-A, K-K, A-Q or K-Q and he may lay down his hand facing a raise.

Turn: Q♣-9♦-6♠-7♥.

Answer 5: (a) 8 (b) 4 (c) 10 (d) 8.

Lo and it came to pass that there was great rejoicing in the camp of Alf. But how can he make the most money here? To win the maximum, it is best to lead out. We must have empathy with our opponents. From Bert's viewpoint, what could be more logical than for his opponent to lead out with a hand such as A-Q after that turn card?

Answer 6: (a) -5 (b) 0 (c) 10.

If you did not get this one right, there is no hope for you at all. The only reason Alf does not have a Weapon of Mass Destruction is that there is only one opponent in the pot. Of course, he could be outdrawn, but as nearly always in poker, if there is no risk, there is probably little profit.

Index of Concepts

Hold'em is very pure form of poker, in which there are many ideas that recur in different scenarios. The reference numbers relate to hand numbers.